ASPECTS OF LINCOLN

ASPECTS OF LINCOLN

DISCOVERING LOCAL HISTORY

Edited by
Andrew Walker

Series Editor
Brian Elliott

Wharncliffe Books

First Published in 2001 by
Wharncliffe Books
an imprint of
Pen and Sword Books Limited,
47 Church Street, Barnsley,
South Yorkshire. S70 2AS

Copyright © Wharncliffe Books

For up-to-date information on other titles produced under the
Wharncliffe imprint, please telephone or write to:

> **Wharncliffe Books**
> **FREEPOST**
> **47 Church Street**
> **Barnsley**
> **South Yorkshire S70 2BR**
> **Telephone (24 hours): 01226 - 734555**

ISBN: 1-903425-04-2

A CIP catalogue record of this book is available from the
British Library

Cover illustration: *A view of Lincoln from Drury Lane,* c.1886, M Clouse, Courtesy of the Usher Gallery.
Copyright reserved, Lincolnshire County Council

Printed in the United Kingdom by
CPI UK

CONTENTS

INTRODUCTION

by Andrew Walker

Lincoln has already been well served by historians, as the contributors to this collection acknowledge. However, there is still scope for much more investigation of Lincoln's rich past. This current volume aims both to entertain and to educate. It has been compiled to appeal both to readers with an interest in and an affection for Lincoln and also to those interested in the subject of Local History more generally. One of the book's aims is to raise as many questions in readers' minds as it answers. It is hoped that it will stimulate more interest in the study of the city and its locality's past – both recent and distant.

Aspects of Lincoln covers a broad time period. Jim Johnston's fascinating metaphorical pub crawl uses probate inventories to help reconstruct the colourful world of Lincoln's seventeenth-century inns and alehouses. The book also examines aspects of the city's history within living memory. Drawing upon his own extensive visual archive of material, George Clarke's richly illustrated examination of the city's twentieth century cinema history will undoubtedly prompt readers' recollections of their own past cinema-going experiences.

Several chapters here draw our attention to prominent Lincoln individuals, who have been rather neglected. John Wilford examines the fascinating and turbulent life of Thomas Watson, Lincoln's last Catholic bishop. John Wilford's chapter highlights the central part played by Thomas Watson, Bishop of Lincoln in the political and religious disputes that raged during the sixteenth century. A little closer to our own times, Alice Rodgers painstakingly records the life of her great aunt, Emily Gilbert. Alice Rodgers' chapter, based on personal recollections and an extensive family archive, reveals clearly how a determined woman could carve out a 'respectable' life for herself outside the confines of the home during the early twentieth century. Jenny Walton's piece examines the role of Lincoln's town crier, making excellent use of an interview with Lincoln's most authoritative voice on the subject – Terry Stubbings, the city's current town crier.

The collection acknowledges the social and economic changes that prompted significant growth in Lincoln during the nineteenth century. By examining a variety of primary source materials including much visual evidence, Dennis Mills traces the development from the late eighteenth century onwards of a Lincoln 'edge-land' neglected by historians, the Witham Valley east of Canwick Road. Kate Hill's stimulating chapter also focuses upon Lincoln during this period of significant social and economic change. The chapter stresses the diverse nature of Victorian middle-class life in Lincoln and suggests that the city's middle classes were slow to embrace civic reform.

John Sanders' chapter also, indirectly, considers nineteenth century middle-class life in Lincoln through an examination of an artist whose work had many middle-class admirers. Peter De Wint's paintings, as John Sanders reveals, drew considerable inspiration from the city and its surroundings. Using examples of De Wint's work in Lincoln's Usher Gallery collection, John Sanders demonstrates persuasively why De Wint's pictures of early nineteenth century Lincoln are of such importance.

Two other chapters within the collection focus upon nineteenth century life within the city. Eleanor Nannestad's work draws upon her impressive knowledge of Lincoln Central Library's Local Studies collection. She demonstrates how increasing wages and leisure time, alongside developments in transport, allowed Lincoln's population to enjoy trips to a variety of destinations during the period. In sharp contrast, Terry Nowell's chapter on Lincoln's prisons, through a close reading of a variety of prison officials' journals, reveals the changing experiences both of inmates and employees of Lincoln's prisons.

Inevitably, Lincoln's past is intimately tied up with that of the nation. In many of the chapters already mentioned, developments in Lincoln are placed in a wider context. Two chapters demonstrate clearly how national events and policies affected local lives during the twentieth century. Philip Swan's chapter looks at how Lincoln and its surrounding airfields responded to the demands of war and the arrival of Bomber Command between 1939 and 1945. With the extensive use of autobiographical, oral and pictorial evidence, he examines the wartime airbase communities that developed in the Lincoln district and their social and cultural impact. Jan Relf's chapter looks at the way in which one educational institution in Lincoln responded to the changing national educational agenda through the twentieth century. Making use of North Lincolnshire College's archives, she carefully plots the development of technical education in the city from the later nineteenth century to the 1990s. Jan Relf's chapter is a timely reminder of the important economic, cultural and social contributions all of Lincoln's educational institutions have made and continue to make to the city.

I would like to record my thanks to the contributors. With their help, the collection bears all the best hallmarks of an *Aspects* volume: carefully researched and readable chapters covering a diverse range of subjects written by authors with evident enthusiasms who are keen to share their findings with others.

On behalf of the contributors, I would also like to express gratitude to the staff of the various archives and libraries who have helped in the production of this volume, but particularly to staff at Lincoln Central Library and Lincoln Archives.

Finally I would like to thank all those at Wharncliffe Books, especially Mike Parsons and Brian Elliott, for their willing help and wise counsel in the production of this work.

1. Dark Skies: Royal Air Force Bomber Command in Lincolnshire

by Philip Swan

SIXTY YEARS AGO, THE SUMMER SKIES of the southern counties of England were filled with the shapes of Hurricanes and Spitfires fighting what came to be called The Battle of Britain. At this time Lincolnshire rural life was still dominated by the agricultural seasons, and on one level appeared to continue as it had for centuries.[1] Yet this was a Total War, which meant that everyone, in their various ways, was involved in the conflict against Fascism. Increased agricultural production[2] was imperative in order to sustain a population which was being denied the importation of commodities from other parts of the world. Lincolnshire was also, however, a stage upon which an important part of Britain's war policy was to be set. The men and women of Royal Air Force Bomber Command were to be the actors who would play out a role which would take the war to the very heart of Nazi Germany.[3]

Figure 1. Lancasters depart from Elsham Wold for a night raid on the Ruhr. Picture issued 1943. *Imperial War Museum. CH. 9029.*

The Royal Air Force had a longstanding presence in Lincolnshire before the outbreak of hostilities in 1939 in that there existed a number of permanent bases. Many of those airfields are still with us, and include RAF Cranwell and RAF Scampton. In 1942 Bomber Command experienced a massive expansion of its offensive capacity with the building of a large number of new airfields – many of these were constructed in Lincolnshire. By 1945 there were nearly fifty Air Force stations, twenty-eight of which were bomber bases, more than in any other county (Figure 1). There are remnants of those old airfields still to be seen scattered every few miles across the Lincolnshire countryside. Some are now derelict, others are used for other purposes, a few are still used for aviation. Amongst those disused airfields are Ludford, Fiskerton, Faldingworth, Bardney, Metheringham - and the list goes on. Those which have found new uses include former RAF Kirmington which now operates as Humberside International Airport. Some such as East Kirkby, Wickenby, Metheringham, Hemswell have museums commemorating their role in the Second World War.

The unprecedented amount of airfield building which took place in the period around 1942 had an impact on the county of Lincolnshire in a variety of ways. The impressive thing is the speed at which these airfields were constructed. An operational airfield is much more than the building of runways and aircraft hangars. These were, in effect, small towns which covered areas of about 600 acres. It is estimated that in total the Lincolnshire airfields covered a staggering 30,000 acres. They required the infrastructure of a small town, including all the usual services of water supply, electricity, gas and sewerage disposal. Jack Currie, who was a Lancaster pilot with 12 Squadron based at RAF Wickenby, describes the bomber base as,

> *a little principality all of its own, its foreign policy was simple enough - attack Germany. That aside there was little that was tremendously exciting. A tiny state without elder statesmen - only the diversions of youth.* [4]

The population for each of the RAF stations was in the thousands – comprising not just air-crew, but large numbers of ground crew and a myriad number of service personnel who contributed to the (fairly) smooth and efficient running of the base. Jack Currie eloquently recounts the numerous day-to-day tasks required in support of the squadron activities:

> *On the technical and flying sites of them all, bombs and pyrotechnics*

were stored, transported and hoisted into bomb-bays; thousands of rounds of .303 bullets were set in ammunition-trays and loaded into turrets; gun-sights were harmonised and bomb-sights levelled; petrol, oil and oxygen were piped into tanks and cylinders; parachutes, Mae Wests, dinghies and escape kits were scrupulously maintained; engines were overhauled, airframes patched and polished, and control-cables greased; hydraulic systems were bled and refurbished; compasses were swung and adjusted, radar sets and instruments were constantly serviced and re-calibrated... runways and taxi-tracks were swept, the systems of flare-path lights, glim-lamps, lead-in lights, Chance lights, gooseneck flares and beacons were checked; fire-engines and ambulances were always at the ready, and Bofors guns were manned. In Station offices and on domestic sites, adjutants wrote letters for the CO's signature to bereaved next-of-kin, dentists pulled teeth, doctors discouraged all forms of disability, chaplains led devotions and dispensed cocoa at de-briefings, clerks kept records, sentries did their duty, cooks did their worst, waitresses waited, batwomen batted, weather forecasters forecast, and orderlies fought their endless battles with disorder. [5]

At any one time there were in the region of 80,000 to 90,000 personnel accommodated on Lincolnshire airfields, which constituted a huge inflow of men and women into this predominantly rural county. These service men and women originated from throughout the nation, the 'overseas dominions', and occupied countries such as Poland. The air-crew of Bomber Command were largely young people in their late teens and early twenties. A few were even younger. Ted Cachart was just 'fifteen and three quarters' when he joined the RAF after 'exaggerating' his age. Whilst on active service and based at RAF Binbrook the Lancaster bomber, in which he was the radio operator, had a mid-air collision with another Lancaster over the target. He successfully parachuted into occupied territory and spent the remainder of the war in a POW camp.

The impact on the life of Lincolnshire must have been fundamental. For instance, the demand for beer in favourite watering places such as the *Saracen's Head* in Lincoln would have been huge. The airfield at Bardney, like others, had an effect on the local area 'it did for the pubs, obviously. They really lapped it up. And the bus companies, there were one or two bus companies who did well...' [6] The RAF stations were not completely self-contained and the 'men (and women) stationed in them did not lead segregated

Figure 2. RAF Wickenby – armourers at the Bomb Dump, 1945. *RAF Wickenby Memorial Museum.*

Figure 3. The Control Tower (Watch Office) RAF Wickenby c1943. *RAF Wickenby Memorial Museum.*

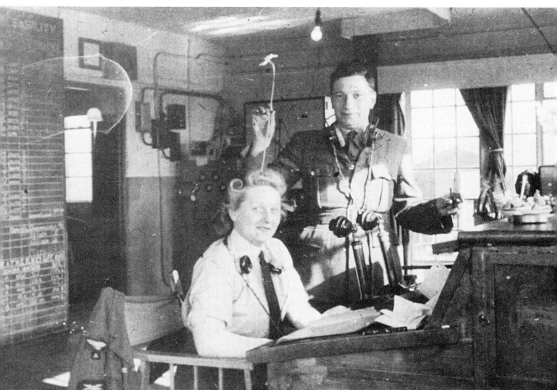

Figure 4. The Control Tower (Watch Office) as it is today. *RAF Wickenby Memorial Museum.*

lives.'[7] Many of them had their own facilities, such as cinemas, gymnasia, NAAFI, and messes, but the off-site amenities, especially the pubs and cinemas of the nearest towns and villages were certainly an attraction which many service men and women preferred. The congregations of local churches were increased, and many attended and became involved in village functions. The young men also 'courted' local girls.[8]

Bill Brown recalls how, 'at the time I was on operations, the average life was three weeks'. The chance of survival for aircrew, statistically, was about one in three – so it comes as no surprise that many young men developed a sense of 'live for today'.

Campbell Muirhead was stationed at RAF Wickenby between 9 May and 19 August 1944, during which time he completed the thirty operations required to finish his tour of duty (Figures 2, 3 and 4). During that short, but intense period, he kept a diary which provides a fascinating insight into day to day life on a Lincolnshire Bomber Command air base. One of the early entries (10 May 1944), after recently arriving at Wickenby, states:

> *Have ascertained two interesting, but somewhat chilling, facts since I arrived here. The first is that, while the operational tour consists of 30 flights over Germany and/or Occupied Europe, the chances of survival are said to be about 30 per cent. Now isn't that a cheerful and heart-warming note on which to get this diary under way...*[9]

Figure 5. Engine startup, Lancaster 'Just Jane' at Lincolnshire Aviation Heritage Centre, East Kirkby. *Philip Swan.*

On joining 12 Squadron at Wickenby in late June, 1943 Jack Currie, aged 22, from London noted that the week preceding his arrival at the station eight Lancasters had failed to return from missions, '...fifty six men had bled, burned and fallen to earth'.[10] On returning from a raid on Germany to the skies of Lincolnshire did not mean the bomber crews were safe – there was always the risk of German 'intruders':

> *they used to come back with us. You would be coming down and you would get a call that there were 'bandits. bandits'. You just imagine, you get somewhere in the region of 600 bombers milling around Lincolnshire... you've all got your lights on... so all the lights go off ... there were mid-air collisions.*[11]

Overall, these were difficult and dangerous times for the aircrew of Bomber Command (Figure 5). Nevertheless, all the RAF personnel found their 'distractions of youth' wherever they could. The evenings when operations were cancelled would see large numbers of young men and women travelling to Lincoln by bus, car, train, bicycle, or on foot. There were special drinking places which Bomber Command veterans still hold in their affections! Those who did not make the trek to Lincoln might frequent local pubs – those stationed at RAF Binbrook *The Marquis of Granby*, or RAF Wickenby, *The White Hart* at Lissington. One evening in October 1944 there was a lull in operations caused by bad weather, and some of the RAF Fulbeck personnel decided to go off base for entertainment. After finding the local pubs closed at Brant Broughton, they went on to Beckingham where they had heard that two pubs were open and there was a dance.

> *The dance was a typical village effort, a small school room being the 'floor'. but there were bags of partners such as they were. Lefty fiddled three eggs out of the raffle and we also got some apples, so we were quite happy.*[12]

On-base drinking, and other social activities, would take place in the mess, with the consequence that '...each (mess) bill invariably seems higher than the previous one... I suppose we all are drinking that little bit more as the tour (of duty) progresses'. (Campbell Muirhead,[13] June, 1944). Spirits would sometimes run high:

> *18th June 1944. Stood-down now ... . [due to bad weather]. So we had a mess 'do' last night. And after about three pints we decided that Vernon would perform the 'black footprints' effort. Vernon wasn't all that enthusiastic... Anyway, we grab Vernon, remove his shoes. Someone fetches a basin into which we pour beer and, strictly according to recipe, mix thoroughly with soot from the ante-room chimney. Into the brew goes Vernon's stockinged feet. Then Horsfall grabs him by one side while I do likewise the other. We lift him. Vernon now accepts the inevitable and jerks both his feet up. We then 'walk' him up one wall, across the ceiling and down the other wall leaving a dirty trail of black footprints.*[13]

Gordon Stooke recalls that the first Australian accents to be heard in the pubs of Binbrook was at the end of April, 1943. This was when an advance party visited the base to make arrangements for the transfer of 460 Squadron, RAAF. from Breighton, near York.

> *Grimsby and Market Rasen were places to visit, but none so popular as The Marquis of Granby pub in Binbrook village. Rene Trevor ran*

> *The Marquis of Granby throughout the war. She was the licensee but found herself thrust into the role of 'mother' to hundreds of young Australian airmen. She sewed on buttons and new decorations, mended jackets and cooked meals for the young men who flew bombers from Binbrook between 1940 and 1945. The youngsters who flew those aircraft never forgot Rene Trevor.*

The war and its impact on the home front had changed life in Britain in so many ways, and perhaps especially for women. Rene Trevor had a family history in the licensed trade when she was growing up - her father was licensee of *The Crown Inn* in Tealby for 43 years. Together with her husband she took on a pub in November 1939. When her husband was posted overseas to the Middle East, she continued to run *The Marquis of Granby* at Binbrook. Rene Trevor remembers the day the Australians moved in:

> *My daughter Anne was about three at the time and we had just begun to tell her about the war and about the Germans. One day she came running in screaming 'Mummy, Mummy, the Germans are here!' She had just heard an Australian accent for the first time.*

Gordon Stooke was one of those young Australian men who experienced the hospitality of *The Marquis of Granby* pub. His own fascinating story of being shot down, his travels through occupied Belgium, and his eventual capture are recounted in his book *Flak and Barbed Wire*. He recalls how,

> *The first airmen to arrive at* The Marquis of Granby *were the crews of the obsolete Fairey Battles. Rene can remember them saying, 'A real English pub with a piano - can you play it?' Rene could, and she could sing too. That started a relationship between* The Granby, *its landlady and the boys of Bomber Command. Songs such as 'Cowboy Joe' and 'Goodnight Sweetheart' were to become familiar at the pub throughout the war years.*

Aircrew would walk or cycle down to *The Granby* every night they could for a pint or two of Holes Ale (later Hewitts, Guinness or whatever else she could obtain) or maybe she would serve her famous meal – sausage, two eggs and toast, for 1s. 6d. For those who survived their tour of duty there would be a party in the back room of *The Granby*, and,

> *one of the traditions at these parties was for the airmen who successfully finished their tour, to be held aloft while they wrote their names on the ceiling of the room. Perhaps those names are still there under several coats of paint.*[14]

Figure 6. Crew briefing, 57 Squadron, East Kirkby. *Lincolnshire Aviation Heritage Centre/Philip Swan.*

Figure 7. Aircrew, 57 Squadron, East Kirkby. *Lincolnshire Aviation Heritage Centre.*

Figure 8. Aircrew, 57 Squadron, East Kirkby. *Lincolnshire Aviation Heritage Centre.*

Figure 9. Ted Cachart, Wireless Operator, 49 Squadron, Fiskerton.
By courtesy of Ted Cachart.

Figure 10. Ted Cachart (back, left) and crew, 49 Squadron, Fiskerton. *By courtesy of Ted Cachart.*

Jack Currie found himself under pressure from one of his crew members not to over-imbibe. In his role as pilot he had a responsibility to his crew, and

> *...the rear gunner only let me drink on stand downs or on leave. On stand downs we would usually go into Lincoln. I suppose we brought the occasional WAAF in here (The* White Hart *at Lissington). None of us were married... but in those early days we were not really interested in beer or WAAFs to be honest, we were only interested in seeing what names were going to be on the Battle Order and what the target was.* [15]

The armed forces comprised young men and women from a variety of social backgrounds, and not surprisingly there was also a variety of experience and social preferences (Figures 6-10). Not all Air Force personnel found their entertainment and distractions in the pubs of Lincoln and Lincolnshire. Pip Beck, who served as a WAAF (Women's Auxiliary Air Force) radio/telephony operator at RAF Waddington and RAF Bardney, recounts the,

> *WVS* [Women's Voluntary Service] *canteen in the august surroundings of the Bishop's Palace... those of us who went there loved it. The rowdier element kept away, and it was quiet, comfortable, and gracious, with chintzy armchairs and polished tables and vases of flowers... Once, feeling energetic, I walked all the way from Waddington to Lincoln, and up the hill to the Bishop's Pal*[ace]*, longing for a cup of tea. This I had, and a couple of jam tarts... I thought I had never tasted anything so good.* [16]

Bill Brown found little time for social activities, simply because of the way his ops fell. He recounted how,

> *on training stations social activities were better than operational because they'd be teaching dance classes or running whist drives. But on an operational squadron the only social activity was in the mess, we used to play housey housey* [bingo] *or anything like that. Because as you can see from my log book I was consistently out nearly every other night, and sometimes consecutively, so there was no time for anything social... On the odd occasions... there was the opportunity to have the day off... .*

The type of social activities would, of course, vary depending upon the person and the circumstances they found themselves in. Bill Brown was lucky to have his 'girl' (future wife) living and working in Lincoln:

she was a duckie on the buses - a conductress on the buses... When I came into Lincoln to see my girl, they used to go down the Jolly Fisherman *or where ever, drinking every night, as a crew like. But of course they had nowhere to go socially, I did. I also had a friend in the village* [Bardney] *who worked on the railway. If ops were cancelled rather late, too late for me to go to Lincoln... I used to go down to Cyril's house, have supper and play a few games of draughts.*

Other favourite pastimes in the war years included going to the cinema and dancing.[17] Going to the 'pictures' had become increasingly popular during the interwar period, and continued to be so during the war. On the eve of the Second World War Lincoln had eight cinemas - The Savoy, the Radion in Newport, the Ritz, the Plaza, and the Central in St Swithin's Square, The Grand, The Regal, and the Exchange Kinema. The Radion was requisitioned by the army, and the Plaza and the Central both burnt down in 1943 and 1944 respectively.[18] A number of war films were produced, often based on real incidents, for example San Demetrio. These and films such as *Mrs. Minever* and Chaplin's *The Great Dictator* had great entertainment value but also served to boost morale.

Cinemas gave much needed entertainment, but they were also a source of news about the war, and made available public service items giving advice on winning the war on the Home Front. Advice such as how to save fuel, how to 'make do and mend', and how to compensate for the shortages of food commodities such as eggs. Much of this information was provided by Pathe and Movietone newsreels, together with items from the Ministry of Information. The latter included the work of the Crown Film Unit, of which perhaps the most well known short film is *Listen to Britain*. The work of director Humphrey Jennings, *Listen to Britain* was, in many ways, a contribution to a wider debate taking place in Britain. Quite early in the war there was a discussion regarding what the people, in this 'People's War', were fighting for, and what would society be like after the war.[19] The general feeling was that there should not be a return to the unemployment and social division of the interwar period. The war, and in particular rationing, had brought about a degree of egalitarianism, or social levelling, never before seen. One of the questions being asked was, why should a fair distribution not continue in peace? It has become something of at truism that the diet of the working classes actually improved under a system of rationing!

Social dancing was another important activity which provided

Figure 11. WAAF ground crew leaving a hangar to service and repair a Stirling bomber just back from a night raid. *Imperial War Museum. CH.13708*

distraction from the problems of war. Dances might be organised on base, or in the local village hall or nearby towns. In terms of the social impact of RAF station dances, this activity was a two way process in that young ladies from the local villages were invited onto the bases to attend. The WAAF contingent on the airfields were outnumbered by the men at a ratio of about 10:1, and in many respects they could be 'picky' about choosing a partner. A former WAAF at RAF Ludford Magna recalls how on being invited to dance by a young airman, the first thing they asked was how many 'ops' he had done. If not well into his tour of duty then it was felt that the odds were not in his favour and the usual response was to decline! She did, however, go on to say that she broke her rule on one occasion, even though the airman in question had not yet completed a single operation - and she is still married to him.

The freedom which the young women experienced was, for many, unprecedented, and the type of work they could do was varied and in some cases very different from what had previously been available, or at least socially acceptable, for women to do (Figure 11). Pat McCarthy wanted to join the WAAFs:

> *What with the boring shop job I was more determined than ever to get into the WAAFs and lead to what I thought was going to be all great fun – dancing all hours, meeting handsome air crews, bags of leave to show off my uniform and my latest young man.*[20]

After failing to be accepted three times because she was too young, she finally achieved success in her application and received a letter asking her to report to Oxford RAF recruitment centre for a medical, which she passed. She was then required to report to camp in Cambridge. At this point she had to decide which trade she wanted to be trained for. Her main criterion for this choice was:

> *I wanted anything which would enable me to be near aircraft… 'Flight Mechanic' was a new trade which not many girls wanted to be – they all went for office or parachute packers, drivers or cooks. They could not have offered me anything better.*[21]

She went on to do her Flight Mechanics training at Hednesford in Staffordshire in 1941. After training she found that:

> *at first it seemed as if we WAAFs got all the rotten dirty jobs like cleaning cowlings with petrol, cleaning the hangar, lying on tails of aircraft while they revved up. Gradually they realised we could do mechanics' jobs… .*[22]

Inevitably, there were liaisons between aircrew and WAAFs:

The other form of amusement on the camp was... the WAAFery. There was a dark eyed girl in the MT section, she was beautiful. But she had bad luck with her boyfriends. A pilot, a gunner, they both went missing. Then she turned her attentions to a civilian the Works Department and he killed himself on a motorcycle. I had a date to meet her... [and] ...there was a tannoy message, my name called all over the camp, ten minutes before I was to due meet her. Report to some other place on the base. I got there, there was nobody there. I found myself in an empty map room, locked in. I got out about an hour later - nobody knew anything about a tannoy call... I hadn't realised what a superstitious lot they [his crew] *were. So I never did lay that jinx.*[23]

A visitor to the RAF Wickenby Memorial Museum commented about a photograph showing the full complement of seven crew members standing in front of their Lancaster. All but one of the crew members are identified on the photograph by name. The reason for the anonymity of one, is that the person in the photograph had been drafted in at the last minute to make up the numbers, seven being a full complement. The actual crew member was otherwise occupied with a WAAF behind a hangar!

Life on the newly built airfields could be harsh, especially in winter. Accommodation was in the ubiquitous Nissen Huts and Maycrete buildings which could be cold and damp. Ludford Magna (renamed by those stationed there as Ludford Magma or Mudford Magna) had a reputation for being cold, wet, and muddy. With a constant lack of coke supplies for the already inadequate stoves, toilet doors were removed for use as firewood. An interview with a former WAAF revealed that it was easier, and quicker, to order new toilet doors from supplies than it was to order coke successfully!

The description of RAF Wickenby by Jack Currie was that it was 'windblown, desolate, miles from anywhere. More or less what we expected'. His recollection is that he was 'usually hungry', and a supply of food comprised 'lots of sausages and baked beans... peas like buckshot – slices of unidentified meat... you needed a good appetite to enjoy it'![24] J Winter recalls that when the squadron moved from Fiskerton, they found that:

Fulbeck [1944] was a bit of a mess, because it had been full of Americans who had been flying Dakotas who had been doing the D-

Figure 12. Lancaster and Spitfire of the Battle of Britain Memorial Flight over Lincolnshire. *Philip Swan*

> *Day operations... it was all Nissen Huts with the old boiler thing in the middle and some-body was the stoker at night in the winter months to keep the place warm.*[25]

The older pre-war airfields, such as Waddington, had much better accommodation. Bill Brown recounts how, 'the billets were marvellous (at Waddington)', where he was accommodated in the peacetime married quarters. Bill was ground crew at that time and went on to train for aircrew at St Athan as a flight engineer and joined IX Squadron at the 'dispersed aerodrome' at Bardney where conditions were different.

Many of those who served with Bomber Command in Lincolnshire have returned to visit almost forgotten places, where they spent such dangerous times in their youth. For many it is the first time they have been in the county since the war, a time when they were fresh faced and young. They come to remember once familiar places and in particular lost friends. They are now elderly men and women who once, long ago, were required to give up their jobs, careers, ambitions, friends and family, for the duration of the war - many also gave up their lives. For Jack Currie, Lincoln Cathedral was, in the Second World War, both 'a symbol of faith in the future... and a link with the past'.

For those who participated in that experience, and for their families, the long-term influence has been tremendous – the result is a strong pride in the Royal Air Force (Figures 12 and 13). There is an equally strong regard and affection for Lincoln and the county of Lincolnshire, an affection which has stood the test of time. The RAF presence continued in Lincolnshire after the Second World War, through the Cold War with the V-Bomber force, and despite cut-backs, up to the present day. The recent history of Lincolnshire is inextricably linked to the Royal Air Force and that history is expressed through the many aviation heritage museums located in the county. Many of those museums have the Second World War as their core subject matter – located as they are on the remains of former Bomber Command airfields. Those museums are a lasting memorial, not to war, but to the sacrifice and tragedy of the war. They also perform an important function as repositories for the memories and artefacts, which in turn provide substance to our understanding of this traumatic period and the fight against fascism in Europe.

Figure 13. Lancaster 'Just Jane' looking forward from the main wing spar. *Philip Swan*

Notes and References

1. In 1901 there were 60,601 people employed in agriculture, forestry and fishing, from a total population of 500,022. This was the largest single category of employment.

2. See B A Holderness. 'Agriculture', in Dennis R Mills (ed.), *Twentieth Century Lincolnshire*, (SLHA, 1989).

3. The discussion regarding the tactical effectiveness or morality of 'area bombing', whilst of interest, is not within the brief of this chapter.

4. Jack Currie, *Lancaster Legend: A pilot's story*, (BBC TV documentary, 1998).

5. Jack Currie, *Battle Under the Moon*, (Air Data Publications, 1995).

6. Bill Brown, interview.

7. B R Hollis, 'The Impact of the Royal Air Force', in Dennis R. Mills (ed), Twentieth Century Lincolnshire, p.139.

8. B R Hollis, 'The Impact of the Royal Air Force'.

9. Campbell Muirhead, *The Diary of a Bomb Aimer*, (Spellmount, 1987).

10. Jack Currie, *Lancaster Legend*.

11. J Winter, interview.

12. John Ward, *Beware of the Dog at War...* .

13. Muirhead, *The Diary of a Bomb Aimer*.

14. Gordon Stooke, internet web site.

15. Jack Currie, *Lancaster Legend*.

16. Pip Beck, *A WAAF in Bomber Command*, (Goodall, 1989).

17. It should be remembered that radio, or rather the wireless, constituted an important source of information and entertainment. In particular, the talks by J B Priestley are said to have had a profound influence on expectations for a post-war society. The comedy entertainment of *ITMA (It's That Man Again)* provided plenty of catch phrases as well as a healthy scepticism of government institutions.

18. Fred Hurt and Joan Barratt, *Lincoln War Diaries*, p.117.

19. For example, *The Beveridge Report* was published in 1942.

20. Pat McCarthy, *Erk in a Skirt*, p.7.

21. McCarthy, *Erk in a Skirt*, p.8.

22. McCarthy, *Erk in a Skirt*, p.29.

23. Jack Currie, *Lancaster Legend*.

24. Jack Currie, *Lancaster Legend*.

25. J Winter, interview.

2. Rembering Those in Lincoln's Prisons, 1774-1872

by Terry Nowell

WHEN JOHN HOWARD FIRST VISITED LINCOLN IN 1774, he found there were two prisons in the city – the County Gaol in the Castle, and the City Gaol in the Stonebow. Howard, who was the Sheriff of Bedfordshire, was compiling a survey of every prison in England and Wales by visiting and recording details of each place, to compare them with the conditions of prisons in his own county. He noted that the County Gaol in the Castle in Lincoln had twenty-two prisoners who were debtors, and eleven who were felons, under the care of the gaoler, one Isaac Wood. The chaplain was the Reverend Mr Simpson, who was paid £40 a year, while the surgeon, a Mr Parnell, received £20 per year. On the other hand, the City Gaol at the Stonebow held three debtors and two felons given in the charge of the gaoler, Francis Toyn, and they were without the care of a

Figure 1. The Stonebow, Lincoln, c.1910. *Author's collection.*

STONEBOW, LINCOLN.

chaplain or a surgeon. A narrow lane, now widened to form Saltergate, ran alongside the prison, and a grated window in the wall enabled prisoners to talk to passers-by and beg for food and drink. There was no court to use for exercise, nor a water supply (Figure 1). A visitor in 1802 said the prisoners were half-starved, half-suffocated, and in a state of continual intoxication. In 1809, the inmates were transferred to a new prison that had been completed near Clasketgate – the Sessions House – and was used until 1878 when all former City Gaol prisoners were transferred to the new County Prison on Greetwell Road.

Howard recorded all this evidence in his book on the *State of the Prisons in England and Wales, with Parliamentary Observations and an Account of Some Foreign Prisons*, published in 1777. Many people believe that it began a process of reform and change in the prison system in England and Wales that culminated a century later in prisons being taken under government control in 1877. This was just a few years after the prison at the Castle had been closed and a new prison opened, on Greetwell Road, in 1872. This is the building still in use today. Probably as a result of Howard's visits and remarks, a new prison was built in 1788, and renovated again in 1848.

A prison was probably first provided in the Castle in 1068, when William I planted a castle, taking over most of the south-west portion of the former Roman legionary fortress. This building then became part of the property of the Earl of Lincoln and became the living quarters for successive sheriffs and their constables, and held the papers that made up the workings of the county. The sheriff was also responsible for keeping the property in good repair.

The running of the County Gaol in 1774 was in the hands of the magistrates for the three divisions of the county – Lindsey, Holland and Kesteven, and the costs were shared amongst these three areas. *The Castle Deeds Grant*, dated 4 May 1814, records that a yearly rent of £40 would be paid for the use of the buildings in the Castle by the county.[1]

There were often disputes between the three benches of the magistrates over the running of the prison. For example, when a new chaplain had to be appointed in 1843, each bench put forward its own candidate. The Reverend John Osmond Dakeyne was proposed by the Reverend Charles Boothby and seconded by General Reeve for Kesteven; the Reverend Henry William Richter proposed by Sir Robert Sheffield Bart., and seconded by George Fiesch Heneage Esq. for Lindsey; and Reverend George Rigg was proposed by Reverend Thomas Fardell and seconded by Samuel Russell Collet

Esq. for Holland. In the election that followed, Mr Richter obtained twenty-one votes and was appointed, Mr Dakeyne gained sixteen votes and Mr Rigg just one vote. Within each division of the county there were also smaller prisons, or 'houses of correction', and each bench tried to keep its house of correction open as long as possible. Throughout the county as a whole, there were nine separate commissions of the peace, and quarter sessions were held in twelve towns.

Mention has already been made of the election of the chaplain in 1843. He was one of the key figures in the prison, along with the governor, also called the keeper and gaoler at various times, and the surgeon. Each of these three officers were obliged to keep a journal which had to be presented to the justices at each quarter sessions to be examined and approved. By 1835, the inspectors were appointed to supervise the work in each establishment. *The Keeper's Journal* for 18 April 1836 records:

> *Captain Williams an Inspector of Prisons, examined the whole of the establishment, and expressed his entire approbation of the very clean state of the Gaol. He informed me that he should have to report to Lord John Russell that two men for trial were placed with two Convicts, and that the men who had been tried and death recorded against them were allowed tobacco, which was contrary to the Gaol Act, and highly improper.* [3]

Even then, little leeway was allowed the keeper – perhaps he thought that some tobacco was the least two condemned men should be allowed! The governor was paid the most, £400 per year in 1824, but he carried the most responsibility for the prisoners in his charge, and also had to employ and pay two turnkeys from his allowance. He also had to be on duty most of the day, unlike the chaplain and surgeon, who only attended for part of each day.

The chaplain was being paid £200 per year in 1824, and he had quite clear duties laid upon him by *Act of Parliament*, which required attendance at certain times, and could be fitted in around parish duties. The *Chaplain's Journal* for 25 October 1823 has as its first entry:

> *Duty performed in the Chapel according to the New Gaol Regulation Act: Prayers, selected from the Liturgy of the Church of England with proper lessons, approved and sanctioned by the Lord Bishop of the Diocese and the Magistrates of the three Divisions of the county, are read by the Chaplain each day at 12 o'clock. On every Sunday and on Christmas Day and Good Friday the appointed Morning and*

Evening services of the Church of England are performed at the hours
of half past nine and two o'clock, and one sermon preached.[4]

The chaplain had to be a clergyman from the Anglican Church. It
was not until the *Prison Ministers Act* of 1863 that Roman Catholic
priests and Methodist clergy were to be appointed by the magistrates.
But an entry for 1831 in the chaplain's report, detailed below,
records that a Roman Catholic priest attended a condemned
prisoner, and in 1860 the governor records that a Wesleyan
Methodist minister, Reverend Weight Shovelton, visited another
condemned man, Thomas Richardson, whose execution was respited
just one day before sentence was due to be carried out.

Mr Edward Franklyn was surgeon when rates were fixed in 1824,
and his pay was £50 a year, out of which he had to find the cost of
any medicines prescribed. Gaol fever was a constant threat at that
time. It was caused by bad drainage, and the fever was no respecter
of persons, often killing judges as well as inmates. As late as 1851,
gaol fever was still prevalent, continuing throughout most of that
year, with peaks on three occasions – early February as the prisoners
were being held for the Winter Assizes, when there were twenty cases;
the middle of July for the Summer Assizes, with fourteen cases
reported; and the beginning of October with sixteen out of the
eighteen crown prisoners reported. The Grainger enquiry found that
the chief cause of the fever was the lack of any effective means of
disposing of the sewage. When the prison was rebuilt in 1848 there
was no effective sewerage in the city and a large cesspit was
constructed. This tank still allowed gas to seep back to the prison
and, in particular, the infirmary.[5]

In addition to the infirmary referred to above, there was also a
chapel. There are details of its construction in a 1790 entry in the
Grand Jury Book:

> *Resolved that a Chappell* [sic] *be fitted up over the four Solitary Cells*
> *in the following Manner (the seats being divided into four classes,*
> *Male Convicts and Non Convicts, Females of those descriptions and*
> *Debtors). The Floor to be of Leeds Common Flag Stone, the walls and*
> *ceiling to be of a two coat drawing. The separation between the*
> *different classes of Felons and Debtors to be plain strong framed*
> *partitions with spikes where necessary. Forms and Kneeling Boards*
> *for the different classes of Prisoners, a plain framed Pulpit and*
> *Reading Desk, a raised Pew for the Gaoler, and the Stair Case to be*
> *of wood except the bottom step which is to be of stone.*[6]

Figure 2. The chapel in Lincoln Castle. *By permission of Lincolnshire County Council.*

Later, when the separate system was introduced in all prisons, a new chapel was added in 1848, after directions from Major Jebb, the Surveyor General of Prisons. Under the separate system, each prisoner was kept in a separate cell, which measured four by two feet, by nine feet high (Figure 2). Whenever prisoners left their cells they had to wear a special cap. This had a peak, with holes through which the wearer could see where he was going, but not the face of any other prisoner. During their exercise period in a large yard to the south of the prison block, prisoners walked together in a circle holding an endless rope knotted at intervals. They had to hold the knots which were spaced to prevent them whispering to the next prisoner. After this exercise period, and twice on Sundays, prisoners attended the chapel for service. Once in their seats they were allowed to remove their caps, as the design of the pews prevented them from seeing anything other than the chaplain in the pulpit. During the period of the separate system all British prison chapels were built in this way. However, as the system fell into disuse, they were all, except Lincoln, converted to traditional seating. Lincoln prison chapel is therefore now unique, though the Victorian prison at Port Arthur, in Tasmania, Australia, has a similar but smaller chapel. This is a replica, the original having been destroyed by fire.

The chapel at Lincoln had 78 enclosed seats for male felons. Female prisoners sat on the front row and the bench at the back was reserved for those condemned to death. Debtors were not subjected to the separate system; males sat in the gallery and the females below. The governor and his family would occupy the seating between the pulpit and the gallery and a curtain was drawn across to prevent those sitting in the gallery and on the governor's pew from seeing the main part of the chapel.

There is another part of the prison complex at the castle that played its part in the nineteenth century and that was Cobb Hall, where public executions took place. Up until 1815, this part of the castle had been derelict, but in that year E J Wilson, a county surveyor, renovated Cobb Hall, and in particular the roof, to provide a site for executions. When needed, a scaffold could be erected which was visible from the streets below by the public. This scaffold was given the name of the 'Long Drop' to distinguish it from the 'Old Drop', which previously stood at the corner of Westgate and Burton Road. Cobb Hall was in use for 42 years from 1817 until 1859. During this period, a total of 38 prisoners were hanged, among them, three women. Public executions were abolished by the *Capital Punishment Amendment Act* of 1868. Priscilla Biggadyke became the first woman to be hanged inside the castle on 28 December 1868 and, at the same time, the last woman to be executed in Lincoln.

In 1831, the prison chaplain, Reverend George Kent wrote the following in his annual report to the justices:

Saturday March 12, 1831. Michael Lundy was executed for Murder, confessing his guilt. He was attended in his religious devotions by a Roman Catholic Priest.

Friday 18 March 1831. John Greenwood was executed for House Breaking, confessing his Guilt. He received the Sacrament with seven other Prisoners on the morning of his Execution.

Friday 22 July 1831. William Hall was executed for the wilful murder of Wm Button, confessing his Guilt. During the time he was under sentence of Death, he was very much troubled, and distressed in his mind, and in his last moments great fearfulness and trembling came upon him. I believe a more distressing and heartbreaking scene never was witnessed.

Friday 29 July 1831. Richard Cooling and Thomas Motley were executed for Arson. Richard Cooling denied the crime for which he suffered, though he acknowledged that he was present when Motley set fire to Mr Cherry's Beast Sheds. Thomas Motley confessed the justice of his sentence and acknowledged that he set fire to Corn and Straw Stacks belonging to Mr Cherry, Mr Thompson and Mr Wilson. It is my duty to state that on these solemn and awful occasions the greatest possible order and regularity prevail, and that the Gaoler and all other officers of the Prison do everything in their power to alleviate the sufferings of the wretched criminals.[7]

In 1824, the gaoler had problems with the execution of one James Wetherill, as his journal records. On 5 August, a respite was received by Mr Merryweather, the then gaoler, to delay the execution of Wetherill for murder, because the prisoner had tried to take his own life, and damaged his trachea. On 17 August, Mr Merryweather was given instructions by the magistrates to fit up in the best manner he could the ground floor room under the execution tower for the dissection of the body of James Wetherill. Because light was needed for this task, the arch above the door was taken out and replaced with a window. This work was finished by 19 August and approved by the surgeons. The execution took place on 20 August and Mr Merryweather reported 'everything connected with it properly done.'[8]

This particular entry reveals much about how condemned prisoners were treated. Execution normally happened within three days of the end of the Assize at which the death sentence had been passed. There was no time for appeal. After death, the body was often used for dissection purposes. Often, the family never received the remains of the deceased. Another entry for July 1831 records that the bodies of Thomas Motley and Richard Cooling were interred in the Keep on the day of their execution.

By 1831, the keeper's journal was recording the names of those prisoners who had been capitally convicted, but had their sentences commuted to transportation to Australia for the term of their natural life. The keeper had to arrange the movement of these prisoners to the disused ships, the hulks, moored off the coast, to hold them until a transport ship was available. Such a case is revealed in the keeper's journal for 13 May 1831:

> *I made arrangements for removing Twelve Male convicts this evening*
> *for the Retribution Hulk at Sheerness in the River Medway. I have this*
> *day received an order for the removal of Martha Hendley, a Convict*
> *under Sentence of Transportation, to be removed on board the ship*
> *Mary lying at Woolwich in the River Thames on or before 30 May.*[9]

From time to time, the governor also had to deal with prisoners
attempting to take their own lives. An entry for 14 March 1857
records:

> *William Leach, convict. Appeared in a very excited state of mind at*
> *7am – sent for the Surgeon who saw him at 8 am. At 11.30 am on*
> *looking through the inspection plate I saw the prisoner fasten his*
> *handkerchief and stock round his neck and endeavour to suspend*
> *himself by the bell handle, but the cotton of the stock gave way. I then*
> *went in and removed from his cell everything likely to afford him*
> *facilities for committing suicide. On visiting Leach at 3.30 pm, I*
> *found him apparently suffering from great mental depression which*
> *was caused by the sentence passed upon him on Thursday viz*
> *Transportation for 25 years. I ordered Leach to be removed to the*
> *Infirmary ward and that Francis Lawrence and John Barker, two*
> *convicted prisoners who associate together, with instructions not at any*
> *time to allow Leach out of their sight, or to do anything to himself.*[10]

By 26 March 1857, Leach was sufficiently recovered, and considered
by the surgeon in a fit state of health. He was again placed in separate
confinement and removed from the infirmary ward to his own cell,
but the warders were given directions to watch the prisoner and, for
the present time, he was to have a gas light at night. By this time, the
separate system was in full operation, as evidenced by Leach's return
to his own cell. Also around this time, a convict, Joseph Ward was
reported by warden Smith for talking to Thomas Linton at the pump.

By this period, transportation had been stopped and had been
replaced by penal servitude. Under this system, prisoners had to
endure a period of up to one year of separate confinement before
proceeding to the longer part of their sentences. In other prisons, but
not at Lincoln, convicts were often put to work on quite meaningless
tasks, such as using the treadmill, or undertaking short drill, which
involved lifting a pile of heavy shot from one place and taking it to
another, then bringing it back again.

The Carnarvon Committee recommended sweeping changes to
the prisons of England and Wales and by 1877 all prisons had come

Figure 3. The Prison on Greetwell Road, c.1910. *Author's collection.*

under the control of central government, thus taking away the local authority of magistrates. This resulted in a uniform system throughout the country. This is no doubt why the new County Prison was built on Greetwell Road in 1872 and was in full use by 1878 (Figure 3).

Notes and References

1. County Archive material Co.C. 1/1/1. *Castle Deeds Grant,* 1814.
2. County Archive material Co.C. 2/4 *Gaol Sessions Minutes Book,* 1842-1849, p. 127.
3. County Archive material Co.C. 5/13, *Keeper's Journal,* 1836-1848.
4. County Archive material Co.C. 5/1/20, *Chaplain's Journal,* 1823-1839.
5. County Archive material Co.C. 5/1/17, *Surgeon's Journal,* 1851-1854.
6. County Archive material Co.C. 2/1, *Grand Jury Book,* 1741-1891, p. 205.
7. County Archive material Co.C. 4/1/5. *Gaol Sessions Papers,* October 1830-October 1831. Chaplain's report, item 349.
8. County Archive material Co.C. 5/1/1, *Gaoler's Journal,* 1824-1831.
9. County Archive material Co.C. 5/1/2, *Keeper's Journal,* 1831-1835.
10. County Archive material Co.C. 5/1/5, *Governor's Journal,* 1856-1860.

3. LINCOLN'S TOWN CRIER

by Jenny Walton

OYEZ! OYEZ! OYEZ!
It all happened here in ten sixty-six,
When William the Conqueror got up to his tricks.
He brought all those Normans for a weekend away,
And the whole blooming lot decided to stay.
He built all those castles all over the land,
But he started off something that I think is grand -
He gave his nightwatchmen the use of a bell,
And said to them: 'Lads, I'll let you all yell.'
He started town criers, so give him a cheer,
If it weren't for William, we wouldn't be here.
GOD SAVE THE QUEEN

THE ABOVE RHYME IS ONE OF MANY WRITTEN by Lincoln's present town crier, Terry Stubbings, and was used when he entered a town criers' competition in Hastings in 1999. There is little doubt that, as the verse decrees, the predecessors of today's town criers did first come into Britain with William, and one can even be seen worked into the Bayeux Tapestry.

However, the office of town crier is believed to have actually evolved from that of night watchman, certainly as far back as Old Testament times. References can be found in Isaiah 21, verse 11 ('He calleth to me out of Seir, Watchman, what of the night, what of the night?'); and in Jeremiah 6, verse 17 ('Also I set watchmen over you, saying, Hearken to the sound of the trumpet...') Further, in Hymn 16 of the New English Hymnal *Wachet auf* also mentions a watchman:

> *Wake, O wake! with tidings thrilling*
> *The watchmen all the airs are filling...*

Verse two continues with the theme: 'Sion hears the watchmen shouting...' According to Psalm 127 verse 2: 'Except the Lord keep the city, the watchman waketh but in vain'.

The post of a watchman was to guard or 'watch' the gates and walls of a town when they were closed for the night. Whilst on duty, he had the power to question all strangers trying to enter, would call the hours of his watch and the time of curfew, and ensure fires in buildings such as bakehouses or dwellings were dampened down safely. This latter task was done with a *couvre feu* – a metal cover whose name came from the Norman-French and evolved into the English 'curfew'. It means 'cover fire' and was not only used as a safety measure but also to prevent light attracting any enemies to the town.

In the days when Greece was a mighty empire, the crier was referred to as the herald, carrying messages that may not have always been good news. Hence the saying: 'Don't shoot the messenger'. No doubt the ability to convey such a message via a strong, clear voice allowed the herald to stand at a distance and make good his escape before he was executed. At the Olympic Games, the heralds would announce results, eventually competing with each other to see who could make the best and loudest proclamation – eventually creating their own type of town crying competitions. The call to attention used by town criers: 'Oyez!' is medieval French-Norman, meaning: 'Hearken!'

'When William the Conqueror came and established himself on this island,' explained Terry,

> *he started to fortify the country, including Lincoln. The building of our castle as we recognise it now was begun in 1068, with entrances at its west and east walls. There were Roman fortifications in more or less the same place, before that. Once the castle was built, the lord of the manor lived in its keep. The rest of his people – soldiers, armourers, fletchers, blacksmith, horsemen, cooks – everyone necessary to look after the castle's main occupants - all lived within the castle walls, along with their families.*

The defensive position of the castle meant that, inevitably, the population outside the walls grew, trading took place and homes were erected. The job of the watchmen (also known as waites), expanded to this ever increasing area, making it necessary for them to be able to raise an alarm in case of fire outbreak, stampeding cattle, a raid by an unfriendly neighbouring baron or invaders from the sea via Brayford Wharf. So they were given a bell and became known as bellmen - giving rise to the saying: 'That face rings a bell'. A comprehensible illustration of their duties can be seen in an order passed in Newbury, Berkshire, in 1649, which said:

> *...for the better preserving the Town from dangers of fire and many*

other great inconveniences that are likely to happen, and for the apprehension of all pilfering rogues and suspicious persons, there should be a Bellman that walks the streets from 9 o'clock in the evening until 5 in the morning, and from 9 o'clock in the morning till 5 in the evening, and shout a distinct and audible noise to give notice as well of the present condition of the weather, as of the time of night, which Bellman is to have 5s a week duly and truly paid by the inhabitants...

It is known that some watchmen used a burgmote horn – usually playing a single note only, but occasionally a simple tune. Probably wearing the colour of their lord of the manor, they also began carrying a sword and/or staff in order to defend themselves.

Such an ability to attract attention inevitably led into calling – or crying – announcements such as the opening of markets, meetings of the Corporation, and other important proclamations held during daylight hours – with the result that the town crier, as he was now usually called, often took on the role of Mayor's Herald. This was often done outside an alehouse, no doubt by arrangement with the alehouse keeper to the benefit of the town crier's purse – after all, discussions concerning an announcement would certainly flow more easily and enthusiastically if accompanied by a jug or two of ale.

After reading his proclamation, the town crier would then nail the scroll prominently on a doorpost for the benefit of those who could read. Thus originated the term: 'posting a notice'. Early newspapers followed in the tradition by calling themselves 'The Post'.

The position of town crier was usually only part-time, so he was able to supplement his income by being available for private commissions, such as broadcasting news about local tradesmen's merchandise. Other research has shown that, throughout the centuries, the crier carried out various duties including that of beadle, bill poster and bill distributor.

'Between 1066 and 1662, there are virtually six hundred years of supposition and guesswork,' said Terry.

Records of town criers are rare. But if you think about it, who would or could write down exactly what their town crier did? We don't make a note in our diaries about the arrival of the post. It's just a normal, everyday occurrence. So was the town crier a part of everyday life.

In 1662, Charles II granted a charter to Lincoln that, amongst other favours, allowed it to continue trading and to continue electing a mayor. In that charter can be seen the first reference to a town crier for the Lincoln community. Terry commented:

Amongst other things, it stated that Lincoln was allowed two shire reeves [sheriffs]; *one sword bearer for the Richard II sword that had been given to Lincoln in 1387 to be carried on special civic occasions; one mace bearer; one crier; one sergeant at the key who was responsible for law and order; four constables and several other inferior officers. Therefore, by the mid-seventeenth century the crier was obviously an important person or he wouldn't have been mentioned in the king's charter.*

A literary reference to a crier can be found in William Shakespeare's *Hamlet*, where the title character instructs the travelling players (Act III, scene II):

Speak the speech, I pray you, as I pronounced it to you, trippingly on the tongue: but if you mouth it, as many of your players do, I had as lief the Town Crier spoke my lines.

Appointed by the lord of the manor, the crier would also perform the duties of a beadle, ordering people to appear at a court summons and, as a church servant, he would give notice of vestry meetings and ensure the townsfolk attended. He also administered parish relief for the poor.

He used his paraclete, or wand, to prod at the populace out of the lord of the manor's pathway, and apprenticed children to tradesmen and women, no doubt profiting financially from so doing. Another 'profitable' task was to act as a 'taster', when alehouses and food suppliers would be obliged to allow him to sample their wares – a good way of filling his stomach at no cost to himself. No one dare refuse him for fear of being accused of concealing something unsavoury about their products, resulting in a session in the stocks.

Before the advent of the police constabulary, the town crier would also act as a law enforcement officer. In this role, he could be called upon to mete out punishment, whether it was a whipping, the public stocks or the ducking stool. He was also in charge of the local gaol, was responsible for ensuring the hangman carried out his duties and, on a happier note, could conduct marriage services for the commoners.

By tradition, a town crier was usually a retired non-commissioned officer who had taken the king's shilling, and his military uniform would be retained for use during his town crying duties. In addition, the lord of the manor would issue him with a coachman's topcoat. Until modern times, criers have always worn the clothing of the period during which they live. By the nineteenth century, most of them wore outfits like those worn by policemen of the day – a top hat and a square-cut tailcoat. To their belts were attached manacles, the keys to the local lock-up and stocks, and a truncheon. Their bells could be used as a mace during fights. Later, they took to wearing their best clothes. Modern town criers, however, now usually uniformly wear the costume of a mid-eighteenth century coachman. These brightly coloured outfits are unmistakable in their splendour although occasionally incorrectly identified as mayoral regalia.

Town criers used to be accompanied by an escort, or bodyguard – after all, the crowds didn't always take too kindly to proclamations of bad news such as a rise in taxes or tolls. The escort was also useful to have close by when the crier collected rents for the lord of the manor, or evicted unsatisfactory tenants. Modern-day criers are usually accompanied by a female 'escort' dressed in the same colour scheme and period of outfit as the crier. Even the women criers – and there are an increasing number who have proven they can hold their own with the men – have an escort, usually their male partner. Terry's escort is his wife, Trish.

As far as Lincoln is concerned. after the 1662 charter, the next known reference to its town crier is in a yearbook for the city, dated 1860. He was Thomas Whalley who lived in Much Lane (at the side of the present Littlewoods store site, running parallel to Guildhall Street). Today, the road is just an alleyway, without any houses.

One gentleman who has been well recorded, though, was John Folley, Lincoln's town crier from 1866 to 1898. A newspaper interviewed Mr Folley's great grand-daughter, Mrs Moir, in 1956 and she was able to bring the character to life.

'In the article, Mrs Moir says that Mr Folley married twice, had two daughters by his first wife and a son and daughter by his second wife,' Terry explained.

> *I also have other information that states he was the father of twenty-eight children in total – so that leaves us with the obvious question: who were the mothers of the other twenty-four?*

This active gentleman with the stentorian voice must have been somewhat droll, too. When, during the latter years of his office, he moved house to Gresham Street (known as Upper Gresham Street in his time) on the western side of the city, he named his new home: *Bell Villa*.

Part of his role included being Sheriff's Officer, Sword Bearer, Mace Bearer, Keeper of the Guildhall, Keeper of the Parish of St Mark's and Mayor's Officer. This latter position appeared to give him an exaggerated sense of his own importance for it was said of him that, on a number of occasions, he would act too familiarly with civic heads and members of the corporation. On the other hand, successive mayors were quick to realise the advantage of befriending Mr Folley if their terms of office were to be comfortable (Figure 1).

He died on 10 May 1898, aged seventy-four, and was buried in Canwick Cemetery on the Washingborough Road, south of the city. Lincoln was presented with a photograph of Mr Folley by his descendants, which is displayed in the city's Guildhall.

It was not until 1989 that Lincoln appointed another town crier, a gentleman by the name of Roger Merrett, Terry's predecessor. He was only able to serve the city for four years, having to leave owing to ill health. The post was advertised again. Terry and fifteen other hopefuls applied. 'Up until then I'd never met a town crier before,' admitted Terry, 'although I knew of them from TV films – Dickensian characters, I thought.'

A two-part assessment was held. The first took the form of an interview held in the boardroom of the *Lincolnshire Echo* newspaper, co-sponsors of the event with BBC Radio Lincolnshire, Lincoln City Council and East Midlands Electricity. The second part involved a competition between the eight finalists at *The Lawn* on 31 July 1994, during a 'Family Fun Weekend'. Helping the judges was Ted Davy, at that time the town crier of Alford, Spilsby and Skegness. He had years of experience behind him and had hosted town crying competitions as well as having personally won numerous prestigious town-crying trophies. Terry recalled:

Before I went in for this, Trish and I speculated long and hard as to whether I should wear some sort of fancy dress. Trish discouraged me; in fact she vetoed the idea. It was probably a good thing, knowing as we do know how accurate the town criers' outfits must be.

The contestants were given a bell which they rang 'as we saw fit'. They were also given a script, written by the *Lincolnshire Echo*. Everyone's script was the same, but it was Terry's delivery that was deemed most

Figure 1. John Folley, Lincoln's town crier from 1866 to 1898.
By courtesy of Museum of Lincolnshire Life

proficient. He walked off with the £200 first prize and title of new town crier for Lincoln.

Next came a visit to the City Hall where his 'terms of employment' were discussed – no salary or retainer, but payment would be given for duties carried out on behalf of the city. It was agreed he could take, or keep on, other employment as long as it did not put his role as a town crier, or the city, into disrepute. Terry actually earns his living as a Grant Assessor for the Energy Efficiency Scheme for the Department of the Environment, Transport and the Regions (DETR).

About a month later, he was fitted out in a suitable town crier outfit. Paid for by East Midlands Electricity and made by Bob Morse, a local theatrical costume tailor, the new town crier for Lincoln had his first important duty to perform – his proclamation of allegiance to the City of Lincoln. This was done in the presence of Councillor Rowland Hurst, the Mayor at that time to whom half Terry's prize money was given for the Mayor's charity.

Within six months or so, Mr Morse was making a matching escort's outfit for Trish. She, too, had been smitten by the magical, theatrical world of town crying. She has accompanied Terry ever since, assisting with all his non-civic duties. Terry admitted:

I didn't really know what I was letting myself in for. I sought the help of Ted Davy and he became an invaluable source of information to

Figure 2. Terry Stubbings at Skegness in his first outfit. *Jenny Walton.*

Figure 3. Terry Stubbings at Spilsby. *Jenny Walton.*

help me fit into my role. It was through him that I was invited to become a member of the Loyal Company of Town Criers (LCTC) – which has members from all over the world.

After a few months, Terry began receiving invitations to competitions all around the country. He attended one in Whitby as an observer in 1994, then entered his first competition in April 1995 at Alford, the home ground of his mentor, Ted Davy. For a time, these competitions were a learning curve, his skills not yet as honed as those of the longer serving and more practised criers. But he learnt well, gradually achieving placings, including many second and third positions. After three years, he was an outright winner – at the Blackpool Championship in July 1997. Since then, Terry has won innumerable trophies of one sort or another. Trish, too, has had her share, achieving nine Best Dressed Escort awards. In 1997, he hosted the British Championships in Lincoln.

Through his involvement with the LCTC, Terry has discovered the camaraderie between town criers everywhere. Even when competing at national and international level, they will still help each other out, especially new criers, passing on tips to help them with both their competitive work and civic duties (Figures 2, 3 and 4). As

Figure 4. A gathering of town criers at Spilsby. Terry Stubbings can be seen third from left on the back row. On the far right is Joe David when he was Her Majesty's crier at the Tower of London. *Jenny Walton.*

Terry explained, 'In fact, I've found the competitions, themselves, valuable improvement platforms – where we all poach good ideas from each other!'

Lincoln's town crier and his escort now have two outfits each. Their first, worn frequently over a five-year period were growing a little tired, so, sponsored by the *Lincolnshire Echo*, Terry had a new one tailored by fellow town crier and expert tailoress, Julie Mitchell of Knutsford, whilst Trish has had another made by Bob Morse, paid for by themselves. They have retained the Lincoln Green colours, but in a slightly different shade Terry's topcoat is made from barathea, a soft fabric of silk and wool, and his new waistcoat is now a very 'loud' Lincolnshire Yellow Belly colour in a softer, fine doeskin (Figure 5).

Terry has 'pretty much a fixed diary every year' as far as his civic duties are concerned. For example, every May, he attends the mayor-making ceremony, and the Mayor's Civic Service; also the switching on of Lincoln's Christmas lights and attending the two local fairs – the spring hiring fair and the autumn Fools' Fair. The latter is derived from the belief that, if at this time of year a person was not employed when everyone was still harvesting, then he or she must be a fool.

As a town crier, Terry also takes on the duties of toastmaster and Master of Ceremonies for all kinds of events. He supports charity events, attends the occasional commercial event where he helps local

Figure 5. Terry and Trish Stubbings taking a break during a competition at Princes Quay, Hull. *Terry Stubbings.*

trade promotions and, of course, he and Trish enter regular competitions worldwide where they act as ambassadors for the city of Lincoln. Terry recollected:

> *Some years ago, I was asked to open a Christmas market in a village near Lincoln, on a very cold Saturday one December. The organiser had arranged for me to be taken around the community in open-topped transport in order to promote the event. I didn't ask what - just presumed it would be something like a pony and trap, a Land Rover, or even a convertible sports car.*

The day arrived and Terry met up with the lady organiser who assured him his transport would be along '...in a minute.' Soon afterwards, he heard a rattling exhaust and a diesel engine. 'It was an old, battered, rusty pick-up truck driven by someone who must have been an octogenarian at least.'

The truck stopped beside the resplendent figure in the eighteenth century Lincoln Green outfit.

'Now, maate, 'em you the town crier?'

Not a bad guess, Terry thought, considering no-one else in the vicinity was dressed so flamboyantly. The elderly gentleman then proceeded to pull a tarpaulin from the back of the truck, stuffing it onto the passenger seat. Thinking this was where he should sit, Terry moved towards the passenger door – only to be firmly directed to the back of the pick-up. There he saw what the tarpaulin had been covering: an aluminium framed, striped garden chair. Terry remembered:

> *He helped me up onto the chair, but when I sat on it the canvas sagged so much I could only just peer out over the sides – as long as I hung on with one hand.*

They set off around the village. Every now and again the truck would stop and, from the cab, Terry would hear: 'Off you go, town crier.'

But the streets remained deserted despite Terry's efforts to clamber out of the back of his transportation, dutifully ring his bell and announce the joys of attending the local Christmas Market before climbing back to his icy cold post. Occasionally, he would see a curtain twitch and a nose pressed against a window pane, eliciting tantalising glimpses of a flickering fire and television screen within the cosy interior.

They wound their way around the streets until, reaching the end of the main village road, the truck suddenly swerved to the right. Terry's chair fell over, throwing him across the floor of the vehicle. His chauffeur had momentarily forgotten he had a passenger.

Eventually, they stopped outside the village hall, allowing Terry to try and revive his frozen self with a warm cup of tea. Terry commented:

Just as I was beginning to relax and feel the blood coursing through my veins again, I heard: 'Right, maate, up you go.' My driver informed me I was committed for another hour and a half. The following year, the lady asked me again – but, to my amazement, I discovered I was already booked for that particular date! However, I did agree to go along about an hour after the opening ceremony had taken place, and announce the arrival of Father Christmas... The same old driver arrived in the same old pick-up, sat in the same place I had the previous year, peering over its sides. But instead of stopping at the grotto, he drove past. I ran after him but he shouted out of the pick-up window: 'Can't turn round, it's a one-way street.'

An avid devotee of his role as ambassador for his home city, Terry prepares a different cry for each place he visits, encouraging prospective visitors to his home city. The following is the one he proclaimed during 2001:

OYEZ OYEZ OYEZ

*The Italians visited Lindum [Lincoln] in seventy AD
and made it a Roman Colony;
Eight hundred years later, the Vikings turned
Lindum Colonia into one of the Five Centres of Daneslaw.
William the Conqueror built a castle and cathedral
which stands high and proud in Lincoln to this day.
Every December, the country's biggest Christmas market
stands in the shadow of those magnificent buildings
and receives two hundred and fifty thousand people in four days.
If they have visited Lincoln, and enjoyed its hospitality,
you should come, too.
Lincoln – England's best kept secret.*

GOD SAVE THE QUEEN.

Acknowledgements

I wish to thank Terry and Trish Stubbings, Lincoln's town crier and escort, for their generous help in the production of this article.

4. GETTING DRUNK IN SEVENTEENTH CENTURY LINCOLN

by Jim Johnston

IT WAS EASY TO GET DRUNK in seventeenth century Lincoln provided you had a few pennies in your purse. How much money you needed to spend depended then, as now, on your capacity to hold liquor and the quality of your tipple. By the end of the century the best and strongest drink was ale, the first wort drawn off in the brewing process and it would have cost 1 1/2d a pint. If you preferred strong beer it would have cost you 1d a pint. If you went for quantity rather than quality there was small beer at 1/2d a pint. The best of these were as strong as modern ales and beers. As the unskilled labourer, if he was lucky enough to be employed 200 days in the year at a shilling a day, would have earned some £10 in a year these costs are not as tempting as they sound.[1]

Much of the evidence which follows comes from probate inventories. These were room by room descriptions and valuations of all the household goods someone had possessed at the time of death.[2] About one in three of the Lincoln inventories record the cheapest way of drinking, brewing your own ale at home. This however required an investment of some £3 for the necessary gear, irrespective of the cost of fuel and malt. As the probate inventories record the possessions of only the wealthiest elite of Lincoln it seems likely that only about one in twenty of the city's households would have brewed their own drink in any quantity. The lucky minority who could do so were committed to an arduous, lengthy and risky process if the quality of their brew was to be palatable. Accidents from heavy loads and open fires and misjudgements of quantities and temperatures were inescapable hazards. The women of a household faced these problems, brewing was their responsibility.

For those who could not brew at home there were alehouses. National calculations suggest an alehouse to every hundred or so inhabitants, which means there could have been 40 in Lincoln in 1700.[3] On inventory evidence they were pretty well indistinguishable from ordinary households. The drinking room had to have a fire but this and the stools, forms, a chair or two and a table were common to both domestic households and alehouses. The presence of casks, empty or full, one had 260 gallons of ale, another with ten beds in one room and exceptional outlay on brewing gear must indicate a few of them and there were slighter hints of the trade in the ale pots and measures, playing tables, the reference to a hanging sign or to chamber pots.[4] The clients gathered in these homely but unpretentious rooms probably on a neighbourhood basis like a present day 'local'. Some probably attracted an occupational or social clientele such as riverside porters or non-conformist groups. In them there was always the opportunity of meeting travellers, especially when the city began to prosper after 1660 – drovers from Scotland, seamen from the boats on the Witham and the constant stream of wanderers with news of far away towns and strange events, whose ability to tell a good story might have earned free pints.

Widows and failed artisans gravitated to the occupation of alehousekeepers. It was not a job that gave security or status unless one had another source of profit as a blacksmith or fellmonger. Only two of them, of the hundreds who operated throughout the century, had the occupation acknowledged in inventory or will, and both of these were late in the century.[5] Their success depended not only on the price and quality of their brew but also on the social skills of the landlord or landlady. Evelyn, the diarist, remembered his visit to Lincoln in 1654 because of an alehouse keeper, a tall woman, six feet two inches in height.

> *comely, well proportioned who kept a very neat and cleane alehouse and got most by peoples coming to see her on account of her height.*[6]

Generally these alehouses were the haunts of those who could not afford a fire or a light in their own rooms, servants, the young and only rarely any who had social pretensions. In 1608 the curate of St Benedict was criticised by his churchwardens for spending too much time in alehouses and other idle places and not enough in the study of divinity.[7]

The city authorities, rightly, viewed alehouses with suspicion as nurseries of dissension, felonies and violence. It was in them that radical or heretical beliefs could be expressed like the profane and irreligious fellow who declared before credible witnesses in an alehouse that St Paul the Apostle was not to be believed, he had not written the truth.[8] There was no system of opening hours and control through licensing was only sporadically efficient. Magistrates could close an establishment for three years or more but their agents, the parish constables, were part-time officials, local to the parish, and given a free pint would have been unlikely to have viewed a gathering

Figure 1. Jollity outside an ale house. *The Roxburge Ballads Vol. IX, p745.*

made up of their neighbours intolerantly. They seem to have operated most officiously with churchwardens in accusing alehouse keepers who allowed drinking and singing during the hours of Sunday services.[9] Such gatherings could get very noisy. The English of the time, if not musical, were much addicted to singing and the sale of ballads suggests a pronounced liking for raucously bellowed, and often bawdy, choruses (Figure 1). Most men carried cudgel, and the late night rowdiness of alehouses encouraged their use.

There are no contemporary accounts of roistering in Lincoln's alehouses but presumably their characteristics were the same nation wide and there survive two vivid descriptions of what they were like. Ned Ward, a proto-tabloid journalist in the period just before newspapers became common, was a self-proclaimed expert on the alehouses, taverns and inns of late seventeenth century London, especially the disreputable ones. He seems to have had a more sensitive nose than many of his contemporaries. He described the entrance to an alehouse down a narrow lane like a burial vault stinking of stale sprats and dirt and the drinking room 'as bad as a ship between decks when the tars are in their hammocks.'[10] Some of Lincoln's drinking contexts would have been no more savoury. Some of the scenes he described have not changed, the noise, the heat, the crush round the bar trying to give an order, the pushing and the peevishness of the frustrated thirsty. At least spitting is uncommon today.[11]

Roger Lowe was a shopkeeper at Ashton-in-Makerfield in Lancashire who was inclined to alcohol and kept a diary between 1663 and 1674.[12] His inclination to alcohol was thoroughly normal. Indeed he claimed he could not trade without drinking. A pint of ale or beer punctuated or culminated every social or commercial interaction in much the same way as a cup of tea or coffee today. Funerals, christenings, weddings and the end of quarrels all required their quota of alcohol. He regularly recorded how much he spent in this way, usually between 4d and 6d with the occasional three-quart or 11d evening. Less regularly he recorded the sad and sickly days that followed.[13] The alehouse also provided the setting for aspects of his involved series of courtships which he described in an uninhibited way as when he recorded after treating Jane Wright to ale

> *I was at this time in a very fair way of pleasing my carnel self for I knew myself acceptable with Emm Porter not withstanding my love was entire to Mary Naylor.*

He married Emm Porter but there were more serious evenings when he and others argued about the meaning of Aesop's Fables and quarrelled sharply over the relative merits of Episcopy and Presbyterianism.[14]

In Lincoln if your social status would have been tainted by

Figure 2. An Inn with a diminutive server. *The Roxburge Ballads Vol. III, p293.*

appearing in an alehouse you would have frequented a tavern, the next rank upwards in the alcoholic hierarchy. In these the middling sort could mix, drink and eat without exposing themselves to the uncouth company of the lower orders. They paid more for this privilege in rather more comfortable surroundings with better food, more formal service and greater deference (Figure 2). Where you drank defined your social status. Of London it was written,

> *The Gentree went to the Kings-Head*
> *The Nobles unto the Crowne,*
> *The Knights went to the Golden Fleece*
> *And the Ploughmen to the Crowne*
> *The Cuckolds went to the Ramme*
> *The Bawds will to the negro goe*
> *And Whores to the Naked Man.*[15]

In Lincoln it was the inns where gentry, nobles and knights could be found. In any decade of the century Lincoln probably had about a dozen inns. At worst they would have been little better than some of the taverns and alehouses. Their owners or tenants increased in wealth, status and respectability as the century progressed. Of the eighteen who can be identified between 1601 and 1647 only three acknowledged or were accorded the title of 'innholder'. Eight out of the fifteen between 1660 and 1700 were given this title. In the earlier period only one inn had furniture and fittings worth more than £100 and only two innkeepers died with assets valued at more than £500. Between 1660 and 1700 seven of the inns had furnishings worth more than £100 and four had total assets in excess of £500. In the century four of the innkeepers were women, two of them widows carrying on their husband's business. Table I illustrates the range of provision in a sample of Lincoln's inns together with their types of major investment.[16]

The valuations for furniture and fittings must be seen in the context where the majority of householders had furnishing worth less than £5. The value of furniture in some of the best bedrooms represented more than a labourer's annual wages. Linen and pewter were essential and expensive adjuncts of an inn's reputation. The most obvious sign of the proliferation of furniture during the century is the increase in the numbers of chairs. If Lincoln's seventeenth century inns were to be star or symbol graded on the lines of modern hostelries such a system could well be based on the number of chairs or chamber pots each boasted.

Table I
Investment and Provision in Six Lincoln Inns

Date	1606	1608	1614	1675	1686	1698
Furniture and fittings (£)	171.74	57.37	74.47	15.73	170.62	270.48
Rooms	17	8	8	5	13	35
Beds	29	10	15	4	16	31
Valuation of best bedroom (£)	20.00	15.00	16.00	2.50	16.33	14.00
Chairs	2	4	3	10	32	131
Linen (£)	20.00	20.10	17.36	2.33	23.45	35.00
Pewter (£)	9.00	2.00	3.00	1.00	?	35.00
Chamber pots	26	-	7	1	11	?
Brewing gear (£)	2.66	2.17	-	4.25	15.50	36.00
Wine (£)	120.00	-	-	-	-	30.00
Ale and beer (£)	-	4.00	-	3.33	11.25	35.00

Most towns develop by expanding outwards with concentric rings of new buildings. Lincoln was eccentric. It was bi-focal. There was the uphill concentration of wealth around the Cathedral and in the Bail where the majority of the ecclesiastical and professional elite lived. Downhill was the commercial centre clustered round the city's seat of government in the Stonebow. Each focus had its grand inn, the *Angel* just north west of the Cathedral and the *Reindeer* near the Stonebow in the parish of St Peter at Arches.[17] Both were centres for much more than convivial drinking. Like town and county halls today they had well furnished committee rooms in which city and county were governed. In the *Angel* you could have paid your Ship Money in the reign of Charles I and seen the commissioners for the Land Tax and Assize judges assembling later in the century.[18] Inns were the centres of communication within the city and enterprising innkeepers naturally exploited this to nourish contacts and accrue profits in many subsidiary and successful ways. They operated as brewers and maltsters and were dealers in corn, fuel, mercery goods and wool.

Technically inns were defined by their right to sell wines. Alehouses had been banned from such provision in 1553. It is an inadequate criterion by which to list Lincoln's inns, only six provide inventory evidence for wine out of the thirty or more that can be identified in the century. Those that do provide evidence of stocks of wine provided a good choice. There was Gasgoigne, Claret and white wine from France, sack, Canary, tent, port and muskadine from the

Iberian Peninsular and the Atlantic Islands. One inn had wine valued at £120 in its cellars, another a fifty gallon hogshead of French wine worth £12.[19] They could be expensive drinks. Some French wine was valued at £1 16s 0d a gallon, Rhenish at £2 6s 0d and muskadine at 7s 0d, sack at 8s 0d, and these were cellar valuations and not what the customer would have been charged.[20] Not all of the wine would have been consumed on the premises. The churchwardens of many rural parishes would have come to these inns to buy their communion wines, the better bottles of sack for the gentry in the front pews and a cheaper claret for the congregation on the forms at the back of the nave.[21]

If the churchwardens had stayed to have a drink in one of the public rooms they would have experienced a ritual of urban sophistication. As they entered,

> *a thing started up, all ribbons, lace and feathers and made such a noise with her bell, and her tongue as bad as half a dozen paper mills.*[22]

This flashily dressed bar maid was summoning the servers to fill their tankards, which seem generally to have held a quart of wine. The servers would do their best to encourage a choice of heavily spiced and more expensive ales if wine was beyond the churchwardens' pocket. By the end of the century these novel barmaids had been joined by such innovations as bottles, corks and screw-pulls as well as slate books to record sales.[23] All these innovations gradually seeped down to taverns and alehouses. By the end of the century some of the latter were beginning to describe themselves as public houses.[24]

As Table I shows innkeepers had to invest heavily in furnishing if they were to attract the patronage of the upper classes. In one inn the valuation of feathers alone in mattresses, pillows and bolsters came to nearly £50.[25] In the first half of the century modest luxuries, rare in rural Lincolnshire, were common in the inns in the shape of warming pans, window curtains and fruit dishes. By the end of the century the best were not only home from home for the gentry but show houses for the latest fashions. They displayed an abundance of looking glasses and pictures, the most fashionable types of furniture like cupboards, Spanish (folding) tables and a multiplicity of chairs in the most expensive forms - cane backed and upholstered in Russian leather and Turkey work.[26] Silver could appear on the dining tables and at least one had a clock.[27] Both the *Angel* and the *Reindeer* could stand comparison in terms of creature comforts with many

London inns.[28] Their bed chambers were given prestigious names many of which linger on as the names of present day public houses, the *Crown, The Mitre, The Red Lion*. Giving inns a flavour of French culture was beyond the skills of two of the inventory scribes. They entitled two rooms as the 'flour de Luce' and the 'fflower Deluce'.[29] Only one of the inns seemed to be child friendly, just one had a children's parlour.[30]

The shrewder innkeepers enhanced their appeal by facilities that converted their inns into seventeenth century equivalents of leisure centres. The greatest attractions were cockfights, a peculiarly English sport according to foreigners. At these matches where pairs of cocks hacked each other to bloody shreds the excitement, noise and frenzied betting attracted crowds from every level of society. Foreigners were amazed at the presence of both rich and poor in the wooden arena around the cockpit. It must have been the only time some of the lower orders of society ventured into the precincts of an inn. More sedately two of the inns had bowling greens by the end of the century and their inventories record rollers and pairs of bowls.[31] In addition there were the games associated with playing tables, such as chess and draughts, as well as cards and marbles. There was always music and singing, not necessarily more seemly than that provided in alehouses and the courtyards that coped with the coaches of the richest visitors provided admirable settings for jugglers, acrobats and theatrical shows - provided the actors had been licensed by the magistrates (Figure 3).

Figure 3. Music while you eat in a tavern or inn – the man at the door could be paying the musician to go away. *The Roxburge Ballads Vol. II, p503.*

Figure 4. A rare print showing a party of women drinking. *The Roxburge Ballads Vol. VI, p465.*

Inventories give plentiful evidence of the physical context of inns but nothing on the quality of service or costs. Probably the two greatest experts on the inns of the century were John Taylor and Celia Fiennes. Taylor, the Water Poet, perambulated England between 1623 and 1653 and commemorated its towns and as frequently their inns in doggerel poetry.[32] Celia Fiennes, an intrepid gentlewoman was one of the first tourists who rode from stately home to stately home punctuating descriptions of them with accounts of inns between 1685 and 1703 (Figure 4).[33]

The extremes of Taylor's experience ranged from the jolly fat innkeepers at Dover to the *Rose and Crown* at Nether Stowey in Somerset. Here an 'Ethiopian army of fleas' kept him awake for hours, then a brawling trio of children and when they slept at dawn the town's dogs kept him awake.[34] Celia Fiennes recorded 'the largest reckoning for almost nothing' at Carlisle, a good 'genteel' inn at Pontefract, a godly landlady at Truro but the southwest ruined by the custom of the country for

> *universall smoking both men, women and children all their pipes of tobacco in their mouths…Which was not delightful to me.*[35]

Surprisingly there is not a single valuation for spirits in any of the
inventories for the inns. There was however ample provision in
Lincoln for those who liked strong liquor. They simply had to look
for the spiral red and white striped pole outside a barber surgeon's
shop instead of an inn sign. Traditionally these shops had dealt with
minor first aid and dentistry as well as shaving and cutting the hair
of male clients. Traditionally too they provided strong waters,
possibly as a mild anaesthetic for their surgical practice. There were
only two recorded in the first half of the century but nine between
1662 and 1684. This increase can be attributed to the general
adoption of wigs by men with any social pretension. They were
expensive items, which needed frequent maintenance in the English
climate. The new generation of barbers contrived to make their shops
convivial meeting places where one could be shaved whilst the wig
was attended, gossip, have a few ounces of blood drawn off if feeling
choleric, have a little musical entertainment from the singer with his
cittern who attended the shop and drink gin. The gin was available
in generous quantities. One barber stocked eight runlets and twenty
gallons of it were valued at £3 6s 8d.[36] In such congenial
surroundings you could decide whether to have a new wig made up
from the display of hair available at £2 10s 0d or buy a second hand
one at 5s 0d.[37]

If the barber shop showed a traditional trade adapting to new lines
with gin and wigs Lincoln had a solitary example of the new fashion
becoming popular in England. It had a coffee shop where the new
craze for hot drinks of coffee, cocoa and tea could be indulged.
William Peart, a gentleman, provided coffee, tobacco and honey in
comfortable surroundings in a house near the Cathedral.[38] If you
were of a generation that considered such new fads as effete he also
provided ale, beer, mead and cider.

Coffee and tea had hardly begun to erode the dominance of ale
and beer as the everyday beverage of the population. Facilities for
drinking in the city were numerous but there seems little social
stigma attached to over drinking. Ecclesiastical and secular courts
record a few accusations against those who were disruptively drunk,
the vast majority of them male, but any assessment of the number of
those who became drunk in the city during the seventeenth century
is impossible. Examples of the dangers of over drinking were very
few, one of them, of Parson Dynocke who left the *Angel* 'in liquor',
stumbled into the well by Exchequer gate and there drowned.[39]

Notes and References

1. D Woodward (1995), *Men at Work*, pp. 173-5, 222, 286. Contemporary usage of the words ale and beer was confused. This confusion has spread to modern historians. The usage here and for the process of brewing is based upon P Sambrook (1996), *Country House Brewing in England 1500-1900*, pp 17-18, 89-113.

2. These inventories are in Lincolnshire Archive Office (Hereafter LAO). Probate inventories associated with wills have the reference prefix Inv, those with the letters of Administration LCC Admons and those proved in the Court of the Dean and Chapter Di.

3. P Clark (1983), *The English Alehouse*, p 44.

4. LAO LCC Admons 1699/54, Inv 165/145; LCC Admons 1661/246, Inv 135/19; LCC Admons 1661/246.

5. LAO LCC Admons 1694/74, Inv 194/106.

6. John Evelyn, *Diary*, ed. W Bray (1889), p 238.

7. LAO Visitations (1608) Vj20 f65.

8. LAO Visitations (1636) Vj29 f131.

9. LAO Visitations (1604) Vj18 f13.

10. Ned Ward, *The London Spy*, ed. A L Hayward (1927), pp 34, 39.

11. Ward, *London Spy*, pp 15-21, 215.

12. *The Diary of Roger Lowe of Ashton-in-Makerfield, Lancashire 1663-74* ed. W L Sachse (1938).

13. Lowe, *Diary*, pp 59,65,73,74.

14. Lowe, *Diary*, P 45,26, 52.

15. *London's Ordinance, The Roxburge Ballads,* ed. W Chappel (1874), Vol. II p 24.

16. LAO 1606 - Inv 101/416, 1608 - Inv 102/266, 1614 - Inv 114/350, 1675 - Di 37/3/28, 1686 - Di 40/2/29, 1698 - Inv 193/394.

17. LAO Inv 193/394, 166/108, 177/141.

18. *Calendar of State Papers Domestic* 1633-4, p 14, LAO Chamberlains' Rolls 1685.

19. LAO Inv 101/416, 177/141, 196/394.

20. LAO Inv 101/416, 177/141.

21. LAO Doddington Pigot Par Doc 7/1, Churchwardens Accounts.

22. Ward, *London Spy*, p 3.

23. Ward, *London Spy*, pp 89-90, 171, 271; LAO Inv 177/141, 193/394.

24. Clark, *English Alehouse*, p 195.

25. LAO Inv 193/394, 194/174.

26. LAO Inv 171/141.

27. LAO Di 40/2/29.

28. Cf. Public Record Office, Prob 4/4419.

29. LAO Inv 168/21, 194/174.

30. LAO Inv 105/177.

31. LAO Inv 176/98.

32. John Taylor, *Travels Through Stuart Britain*, ed. J Chandler (1999).

33. Celia Fiennes, *The Journeys*, ed. C Morris (1947).

34. Taylor, *Travels*, pp 104-5, 228-9.

35. Fiennes, *Journeys*, pp 94, 203, 256, 266.

36. LAO Inv 174/138, 148/176.

37. LAO Di 39/2/50.

38. LAO Di 39/2/53.

39. *Letters and Papers of the Banks Family*, ed. J W E Hill (1952) Lincoln Record Society Vol. 45 p 177.

5. VISUALISING LINCOLN, THE WORK OF PETER DE WINT

by John Sanders

SINCE THE MID-EIGHTEENTH CENTURY Lincoln and Lincolnshire have been associated with the work of a number of eminent artists besides Peter De Wint. George Stubbs, 1726-1806, perhaps the greatest exponent of anatomical paintings, especially that of the horse, enjoyed the patronage of Lady Nelthorpe of Scawby. William Hilton RA, 1786-1839, the son of a Newark artist, who was born in Lincoln and lived in Drury Lane, was a history painter who became Keeper of the Royal Academy in 1827. Frank Bramley RA, 1857-1915, who was born in Sibsey near Boston and studied at the newly-formed (in 1863) Lincoln School of Art in 1874, became one of the founder members of the short-lived Newlyn School, Cornwall, which was known for its truthfulness and naturalism, blessed as the place is by good light. William Logsdail, 1859-1944, also studied at the Lincoln School of Art and was a national prizewinner at the Department of Science in London. His studies of Venice display beautiful draughtsmanship, almost photographic in their detailed depiction of people engaged with their environment. He sold *The Piazza of St Martin's*, Venice to J Ruston of Lincoln for the not inconsiderable sum of £1000. Charles Haslewood Shannon RA, 1863-1937, who was born in Quarrington near Sleaford, was an exponent of beautiful books as art, such as *The Pageant* (1896-7), which was rooted in the work of William Morris. He collaborated with Charles Ricketts to produce the occasional journal *The Dial* (1889-97), and the title page of Oscar Wilde's *A House of Pomegranates* in 1891.

Other painters have depicted Lincoln with consummate skill. Thomas Girtin's *Lincoln Cathedral* (with spires), painted from Drury Lane, was probably the inspiration for De Wint's picture painted from a very similar viewpoint, given that De Wint was a known admirer of his work. This picture is displayed in the Usher Art Gallery, Lincoln, as is the great Turner's *Lincoln* (1802-3), a panoramic view looking across the Brayford to the Cathedral. Girtin and Turner were two of the most influential watercolourists of their day. Samuel Prout's *Glory Hole, Lincoln* and Frederick Nash's *Old*

Bishop's Palace, Lincoln, can also be seen at the Usher Gallery. Both Prout and Nash were contemporaries of De Wint. Earlier in time is Joseph Baker's *View of Lincoln Cathedral from the West* (c1742), a flat, formal composition, and the curious *View of St Mary's Bridge, the Cathedral, Castle and St Martin's Church*, Lincoln by John Claude Nattes, c1796, which has flat plates of colour in the later Japanese mode. Later in time are E J Niemann's *Lincoln from Brayford* and John Wilson Carmichael's *The Brayford Pool and Lincoln Cathedral*, both c1858, the former more De Wint, the latter almost photographic in its attention to detail. Later still are works by Clouse (see front cover), Albert Goodwin and Ian Houston's *Lincoln Cathedral from the Meadows* (c. 1965), painted from a vantage point near Washingborough which Peter De Wint also favoured.

Of course, painters continue to paint Lincoln and its environs today, such as John Bangay and David Cuppleditch, to name but two, who, with the advantages of modern technology, can meet the seemingly ever-increasing demand for representations of our favourite views on placemats, teatowels and cameos of all shapes and sizes, which technology, if it had been available to De Wint, would have undoubtedly made him a very rich man, given his sound appreciation of all things financial. De Wint, more than any other painter, is the painter of Lincoln, capturing the mood and feel for the place in panoramic and timeless views of an ancient city perched on a hill. With a little imagination, his compositions can quite easily be conjured up today, as his *Lincoln from Washingborough* illustrates (compare Figure 1, and my photograph, Figure 2). This depicts the cathedral high on the hill overlooking the straggling town below, complete with factory chimney belching smoke, (tempering the bucolic vision), boats on the river and people relaxing in the foreground to give some sense of scale to this living landscape.

Peter De Wint, 1784-1849, was born in Stone, Staffordshire, the fourth son of a Dutch-American father, descendant of the De Windt's family who were wealthy Dutch merchants, and a Scottish mother. He was destined for the medical profession, like his father, until he prevailed upon the latter to allow him to pursue his first love, painting. He was apprenticed to John Raphael Smith of London in 1802, an engraver of some stature, who was an acquaintance of George Morley and patron of both Girtin and Turner. During his apprenticeship he met William Hilton, who was to become his lifelong friend. Indeed, such was their friendship, even at the beginning, that De Wint was briefly imprisoned for breaking the terms of his apprenticeship by not saying where Hilton had

Figure 1. Peter De Wint, *Lincoln from Washingborough*, c1837.

Figure 2. Photograph of Lincoln from Washingborough, 2001. *John Sanders.*

absconded to on one occasion (Hilton had gone back home to Lincoln). However, this incident did not stop his artistic progress, leaving his apprenticeship two years early, on condition that he provided John Raphael Smith with eighteen paintings in oils and water-colours between 1806-9. This he dutifully did. Both the apprenticeship indenture and the letter of release can be seen in the Usher Gallery, as can the enlistment card into the Volunteer Battalion of St Margaret and St John, which De Wint joined, together with Hilton, whilst still apprenticed to Raphael. He met Munro, patron of Turner, Cozens and Girtin, in 1806; and it was Girtin who most influenced his composition. He was also advised by Varley at this time, whose house he lived in, together with Hilton, and it was also in 1806 that he first visited Lincoln, needless to say, with Hilton. He became a student of the Royal Academy in March 1809 (his admittance card is in the Usher Gallery). He exhibited there as early as 1807, *High Tor, Matlock* being one of three compositions submitted. De Wint was admitted to its life school in 1811, and was signed in by the great John Henry Fuseli, Professor of Painting there, and one of the leading Romantic painters of the day, whose fusion of styles could be almost 'Gothic', as his painting *The Nightmare* demonstrates. De Wint also exhibited at the Old Watercolour Society in 1810-11, becoming an associate there in 1810, and an elected member in 1825. The society split over the inclusion of oil painters, De Wint being at its last meeting. Whilst exhibiting at the new society, he did not become a member.

De Wint was a prolific painter, exhibiting 326 paintings between 1807 and 1849. The majority of these were displayed at the Old Watercolour Society. In 1850 his widow sold 493 pictures at Christies, where they fetched £2364 7s 6d. Further major sales followed in 1876, 1904 (when his work was fetching ten times the amounts achieved during his lifetime), and 1941. Twenty-three paintings were bequeathed to the National Gallery, and others went to the Victoria and Albert Museum. De Wint collections are now in every major (and many a provincial) city in the country, with 62 works in the Cambridge Fitzwilliam, the third largest collection after the Courtauld Institute of Art in London, and Lincoln's Usher Art Gallery. There is even a significant collection in Dublin and in the USA, in the Yale Center for British Art.

De Wint was a conventional family man who made steady progress in an uneventful and unexciting way. He was a man of ill-temper at times, who could be difficult, arrogant almost, stand-offish, religious and careful with money. He was a Tory, like Constable, though not

Figure 3. Portraits of John and Harriet De Wint. *Reproduced from W. Armstrong, Memoir of Peter De Wint, Macmillan, London 1888. (Artist unknown)*

of tradestock, as were Constable, Turner, Cox and Cotman, yet he produced daring and unconventional art (as did Constable), choosing the financially precarious yet increasingly fashionable landscape painting. He created timeless compositions of lasting beauty, which sets him apart from Turner, Girtin (who was probably a more influential figure in English painting than the former, if less spectacular) and Cox, who, together with Cotman comprised the English school of watercolour painting between 1775 and 1850.

Compared with the financially lucrative topographical work, landscape painting was a precarious profession. However, the readiness of De Wint's master, John Raphael Smith, to accept his paintings in lieu of service indicates the high standard of work De Wint had attained by 1806. In June 1810, De Wint married Harriet Hilton, at a time when his reputation was growing, and he was receiving much critical acclaim. Harriet's parental home on Drury Lane, Lincoln became their summer residence, an 'escape' from London (Figure 3).

De Wint's early work is akin to Cox and Cotman, and he bears comparison with Turner for a work such as Chester. In works like *House Among Trees* and *The Wayside*, he surpassed Constable, who admired and bought his work, for example *View of the Severn,*

Figure 4. Peter De Wint, *Lincolnshire Landscape,* c1815.

Shropshire in 1843. He was a successful teacher, which was just as well as his chosen metier, watercolours, was financially precarious when he first started. However, he became prosperous, counting among his patrons the Earl of Lonsdale, the Earl of Powis and the Marquis of Ailesbury.

His early work was often in sepia tones, sometimes comprising still life subjects. His technique was restrained, becoming freer in time, with the development of colour. However, his *Westminster Palace, Hall and Abbey,* exhibited at the Gallery of Associated Artists in Water Colours in 1808, was criticised at the time for being too simple by the Examiner, yet he was praised as being akin to Turner for his *View of Lincoln, effect of early hours of morning* by the *Beau Monde*. Ruskin's critique is somewhat patronising, but he was praised by Thackeray.

He was unappreciated in oils in his lifetime, except by his master, Smith. De Wint's oil painting *Lincolnshire Landscape,*[1] c1815, (Figure 4) which is a view near Horncastle, rich in yellows and browns, with a 'big sky', is one of his best. De Wint's landscape oil paintings constitute versions of 'Olde England' which are conservative, and can be seen as a reaction to the French Revolution and Napoleon. Further examples of this bucolic vision are listed in the notes.[2]

He could be almost impressionistic at times, as can be seen in the 'unfinished' *Lincoln Cathedral from Drury Lane* and *Lincoln from South East*, a view from Washingborough (both of which are in the Usher Gallery). De Wint's *A Drover at the Edge of a Wood*, c1830, (Figure 5) painted in oils, is another view possibly from Washingborough, though curiously, if it is, and the angle of the hillside would indicate that it is, the two towers of the west front of the cathedral, which casts an ethereal presence over the picture, cannot be seen from such a vantage point. This impressionistic effect was achieved by building up masses and tones by superimposing layers of colour, bold blots over swift single washes, suggesting form and colour, using large brushes and thick paper, achieving fresh and rich results, often blues, greens, browns and oranges (from a palette of ten pigments, against Girtin's fifteen), favouring landscapes of rivers and harvest scenes. De Wint especially liked the Trent and the

Figure 5. Peter De Wint, *A Drover at the Edge of a Wood*, c1830. *Copyright reserved, Lincolnshire County Council.*

Thames, but also the very different rivers Wharfe, Lowther and Dart. He discovered Wales in later life, but was unimpressed with his single visit abroad, to Normandy. His was a Romantic bucolic vision:

> *Castles, high above valleys and winding rivers; cottages, barns and haystacks nestling comfortably under trees; the rich red of old bricks; cattle pasturing in lush meadowland; church spire or cathedral tower rising above ancient roofs; the illimitable spaciousness of the fens...* [3]

Although he could be guilty of overworking some of his larger canvasses, his smaller works are fresher and more vigorous. His *Potter Gate, Lincoln* is rich and mellow; *Fen Country* has lateral immensity, painted as it is from a horizontal scheme, as is *A Road in Yorkshire*, which manages to combine both Constable and Girtin. According to Martin Hardie he is 'a genius',[4] a technician who created living landscapes, communicating feeling, and for whom:

> *No other painter has ever put on paper with more effect that touch of fine colour from a full-flowing brush, which, as it dries out, transparent and rich in bloom, is the essence of the art of watercolour.* [5]

A painter of the fecund earth, De Wint's range encapsulated engravings for George Ormerod's *History of Cheshire*, published in 1819, John Clare's *Shepherd's Calendar*, Thomas Gray's *Elegy written in a country churchyard* (1849 edition), and Sir Walter Scott's *The Waverley Novels*,[6] as well as the delicate *Girl with Bucket, and a Boy*, the Romantic vision of *Lowther* (1839), and the 'classic' *Cottage at Aldbury*, the last two of which can be seen in the Usher Gallery. His *Sea Piece With Three Vessels in a Breeze* has a delicate touch, though having little love for the sea, as does *Thames Barges* (also on view in the Usher Gallery). *Coast Scene* gives us action frozen in time, rather in the manner of Wordsworth's *The Prelude* (the vision of children skating on the ice). *Waltham Abbey* and *Sketch of a Boy Seated* are impressionistic, *A Lane with Cottages* almost modernistic, whilst his *Thorpe-on-the-Hill, Lincolnshire*, (again, in the Usher Gallery) is Turneresque, and his *Landscape with Windmill* is a rather heavy oil painting. *On the Trent, near Burton Joyce, Nottingham* is panoramic, in the manner of Girtin; and *Stockport* (a commission), is a rare Dickensian vision of the city.

The Romantic view of painting was 'against the rules', depicting Nature not 'classic' views in the tradition of Claude Lorrain, 1600-1682, who painted dreamlike, idyllic pictures of the Roman Campagna, imbuing them with a poetic and nostalgic presence of antiquity. Such was his influence that real scenes were judged by his standards, and gardens were 'landscaped' to be 'picturesque', planned to look unplanned. *Landscape with sacrifice* to Apollo, 1662, is a fine example of his technique. De Wint produced many examples of this Romantic genre: *Near Matlock, Derbyshire* and *A View of Snowdon*; ruins of castles such as Newark and Torksey, (see *Torksey Castle on the Trent, Lincolnshire* and *Torksey Castle,* an unfinished sketch, in the Usher Gallery, the latter, in particular, looking as if it had only been painted yesterday); ruins of abbeys such as Bolton Abbey; and studies of trees which are almost ghoulish or 'Gothic'. For the Romantics, often sketching *en plein air,* the manner of painting became as important as the subject matter. For De Wint, landscapes were of a bountiful nature. They were nostalgic visions showing the continuity of nature, with little evidence of hardship, except perhaps *A Threshing Machine* painted c1830 at the height of the Swing riots. Man, nature and society were to be seen in harmony.

Whilst this conservatism forms the social commentary to his work, the manipulation of the medium is radical, almost abstract at times, with form and colour taking over from the subject. Watercolours lend themselves to the fortuitous or accidental results so loved by the Romantics, helped by wet paper and thick paint, avoiding unnecessary detail, preferring the wider vision and the overall effect. This allowed the observer to participate in the vision, thus completing the dialectic of art: artist, subject and viewer combining to create the finished product. The artist and subject are socially related, as the monographs by John Ellis, which look at the cultural and socio-economic context of some of De Wint's work, demonstrate.[7]

De Wint's is not the idealised vision of Claude Lorrain, but the landscape in the raw, fresh and lived in, a living landscape. He is part of a long tradition in landscape painting, starting perhaps with the topographical work of Paul Saudby's *Roadway through Windsor Forest.* De Wint was probably familiar with Alexander Cozens' treatise *A New Method of Assisting the Invention in Drawing*, which called for invention not naturalism, and is typified by his painting *The Banks of a Lake.* He was also influenced by the landscape painting of Thomas Gainsborough. Of De Wint's contemporaries, Cotman was less detached in his style, and Cox was probably a superior oil painter. Turner obviously stands out because of the audacity of his vision and the atmospheric nature of much of his work, but his *The Pass of the St Gothard* is not unlike a De Wint. And whilst Constable is undoubtedly the pre-eminent oil painter of his generation, it would be fair to say that De Wint could match him at watercolours.

Much has been made of the 'unfinished' nature of De Wint's work because of his known preference for working out of doors. However, it was common practice to make chalk drawings on the spot which were then used in the studio to produce the finished painting. Given that De Wint continued to use hard cakes of paint, not the more modern moist colours, which worked against outdoors painting, he was either a very patient man who applied his materials with unstinting hard work, or myth-making is at work to protect the Romantic image of the artist *en plein air.* Whatever, there is no doubting the freshness of his work, whether painted out of doors or in the studio. If the latter, then De Wint was a master technician who thoroughly understood the materials he was working with. What is known of his technique is that he liked to flood his paper, looking for colour and tone in search of the broader picture, not the detail, to capture the feeling of a view. He had an 'ability to recreate the sparkle of living nature'.[8] His painterly gestural approach was most suited to landscape. His use of damp paper added to the unpredictability of the end result. He preferred to use one unbroken

Figure 6. Peter De Wint, *Lincoln from the South*, c1824. *Copyright reserved, Lincolnshire County Council.*

wash, giving freshness, trusting to chance elements, using colour as a non-descriptive medium. By 1812 his style was established, a free technique within the visual structure. To De Wint, sense of place was more important than the depiction of a 'classic view'. Mood and atmosphere were also important, investing his work with a moral tone, almost. The choice of panoramic vista added to a sense of the onlooker being involved (Figure 6). Girtin was perhaps more accurate in detail than De Wint, who reduced rather than added, whose figures acted as colour accents within the overall composition. He was a conservative Romantic believing in the continuity of institutions, for example, cathedrals, castles and country houses, and the productivity of haymaking and harvesting: this was a nostalgic vision which, nevertheless, extended the limits of watercolour to an almost abstract level, for example, *Sketch: Trees and Boat on a River*.

He often acted as his own dealer, having enviable private patronage, bucking the trend, from aristocrats, the military, the church, perhaps even Coleridge and Queen Victoria. He was successful, if not spectacular: his recorded sales were £356 in 1827, £500 in 1835 and £2000 in 1843, to say nothing of his unrecorded sales, topographical work and flourishing teaching practice.

De Wint did not sign or date his works, preferring his art to do the talking, which makes verification of his paintings difficult, especially as he had over fifty pupils, most of them women, with many aristocrats, and many admirers who imitated his style. The followers he inspired included: John Flower (*Barges by a River's Edge*), who was taught by him; Henry Barlow Carter (*Tattershall Castle, Lincolnshire*), who bought his work; Samuel Austin, who was taught by him and bought his work, (De Wint's influence upon Austin is revealed in Austin's *Gresford, Denbighshire*, which can be seen in the Usher Gallery); John Moyer Heathcote, perhaps the best of his pupils, although on the evidence of his *Windmill in a Landscape*, on display in the Usher Gallery, that is hard to believe; and the Reverend Charles Pratt Terriott (another pupil), whose *Old Hall, Gainsborough* is in the style of De Wint's *Crowland Abbey*, but more detailed.[9]

De Wint was more at ease with literary figures such as Thomas De Quincey, John Keats and John Clare, than he was with his fellow artists, although he was friendly with Constable, who wrote to him in August 1831, describing him as a 'brother in landscape'.[10] He was employed by Taylor and Hersey, publishers of both Keats (whom he met in 1818, contributing to a fund to look after him whilst he was dying in Rome), and Clare (whom he met in 1820). As with Clare, De Wint could make the ordinary interesting, but the former was more aware of the social inequalities of the time. De Wint was, essentially, an urban man. His views of the country are picturesque and redolent with optimistic bounty. He drew the frontispiece for Clare's *Shepherd's Calendar*, and helped to maintain him in High Beech Asylum, belying De Wint's oft-quoted meanness, although he never answered Clare's request of December 1829 for a painting to go alongside the one provided by his friend, Hilton.[11] For his part, Clare wrote a sonnet to De Wint in his *Rural Muse* of 1835.

De Wint possessed the spontaneity and richness to rival Turner, particularly in his purity of form. He did not confront social issues, rather, his vision is nostalgic and bucolic, but he is original in both style and technique. He was interested in the medium of painting itself, which, ultimately, leads to abstraction: the visual experiences, for him, were more important than the subject, for which he was criticised by the *Athenaeum* in 1837, putting the means before the subject –

> *No manipulator of the watercolour brush fixed with simpler, more direct realism masses of foliage, wide fields, proud buildings, nestling cottages, flowing water; and the inborn poetry which resides in every true artist reveals itself in the criss-crossing vivacity and flight of fancy of the brush strokes. De Wint's brush strokes are like dragonflies skimming the solemn well of truth.*[12]

According to Sir Walter Armstrong, it could only have been his love of Harriet that could have inspired De Wint to paint Lincoln so often, accounting for ten per cent of his listed works, which seems rather patronising of Lincoln! Armstrong noted that:

> *In spite of the superbly placed cathedral and the picturesque irregularity of the streets clustered in its shadow, of the city 'above hill', as those who live among its narrow ways so religiously call it, Lincoln is not rich in subjects for the painter. The upper town is small and soon exhausted. The pictorial value of 'below hill' lies almost entirely in the contrast it offers to the stately bulk of the church which rises beyond; while the neighbourhood, as far as the eye can reach, is a dead level of heavy clays, intersected by dykes, and but little enriched with timber.*[13]

Despite this somewhat back-handed compliment, Armstrong maintained that De Wint painted with 'the balance of a Claude and the dignity of a Girtin'.[14] He was a supreme colourist, matched only by Constable, a painter's painter, an observer, a painter of the whole – a view with which his widow concurred, but in more glowing terms:

Most of his early and valuable studies were made at Lincoln and the
neighbourhood, where he ever found new beauties and subjects, and
what a commonplace observer would consider flat and meaningless
was in his eyes highly picturesque. The long, extensive distances with
their varying effects, the flats bordering the river, covered with cattle,
the groups of vessels in the Brayford, the cornfields and hayfields, and
above all the magnificent cathedral seen from so many points, afforded
him unceasing delight.[15]

He was a master technician who rarely over-painted: a great
interpreter of the feeling of a vision – and we can agree with his
widow that 'there is a truthfulness in his scenes which scarcely ever
fails to give satisfaction'.[16]

Despite the often conservative nature of his subject matter, De
Wint's execution of the same was nearly always radical, so that,
artistically speaking, he was very much a man of his exciting times,
and that is, a Romantic. In both his medium and his technique he
was prepared to challenge what had gone before him. At his best, his
compositions are timeless evocations of a landscape slow to change,
almost impressionistic in effect, which allow the onlooker to enter the
contemplative vision of the artist, to feel the moment and share the
almost dream-like reverie.[17]

Notes and references

1. This painting is titled *Lincolnshire Cornfield* in the Usher Gallery.
2. *Landscape with Church* and *Cattle Watering* are further examples of De Wint's bucolic vision, as is his *Driving Cattle by a Hamlet in the Lincolnshire Wolds*, which is full of movement, and akin to Constable, as are *The Saw Pit* and *A Timber Yard*.
3. Martin Hardie, *Water-colour Painting in Britain, II The Romantic Period*, eds. Dudley Snelgrave, Jonathan Mayne and Basil Taylor, pub. B T Batsford, London, 1967, p 211.
4. Hardie, *Water-colour Painting*, p 216.
5. Hardie, *Water-colour Painting*, p 221.
6. Engravings also featured in: W B Cooke, *Picturesque Views on the Southern Coast of England* (1826); Tillotson, *New Waverley Album*; W and T Radclyffe, *Graphic Illustrations to Warwickshire*; and C Heath, *Views of London*.
7. John Ellis, *A Topographical Landscape by Peter de Wint, OWS* (1784-1849): *The Cultural and Socio-economic Context*, which amounts to an essay on Tennyson and the social milieu of farming; and *Peter de Wint, Walter Christaller and the Carrier's cart*, which focusses on the economy of Spilsby.
8. Hammond Smith, *Peter De Wint*, 1784-1849, F Lewis, London, 1982, p 49.
9. James Price, William Lake Price, James Orrock, Thomas Collier, G P Campion, W L Leitch, Wimperis and Hayes were also followers of De Wint.
10. This letter is in the Usher Gallery collection.
11. Clare's letter to De Wint is in the Usher Gallery.
12. Hammond Smith, *Peter De Wint*, p 5, quoting Pierre Jeanneret in the *Daily Mail*, 21 October 1937, from a review of the Usher Gallery exhibition of that year.
13. Sir Walter Armstrong, *Memoir of Peter de Wint*, Macmillan, London, 1888, p 12.
14. Armstrong, *Memoir of Peter De Wint*, p 15.
15. Harriet De Wint, *A Short Memoir of Peter de Wint and William Hilton, RA*, unpub., p 20.
16. Harriet De Wint, *A Short Memoir*, p 29.

17. Other paintings of Lincoln by De Wint (some of which are undated because he did not always date his work), not referred to in the text include:

Lincoln Cathedral from the Castle, 1811.

Lincoln, Old Houses on the High Bridge.

Lincoln from the South. This is a panoramic view looking down Pelham Bridge from Canwick Hill, formerly Little Bargate, in the Usher Gallery.

A View of Lincoln from the South at Little Bargate, c. 1824. This is painted from the same vantage point as the picture above, but either the rendition and/or its current condition is inferior. This is also in the Usher Gallery.

Priory Gate, Lincoln. This was demolished in 1815. This painting is in the Usher Gallery.

Exchequergate, Lincoln, Looking to Castle Hill. This is very similar today.

Newport Arch, Lincoln. This is also very similar today. It is an inferior oil painting. It can be seen in the Usher Gallery.

Lincoln from Sincil Dyke.

Horses Watering at a Farm, Lincoln. This is typical of De Wint's bucolic vision.

Lincoln Cathedral from the River. This is a panoramic view subordinating the Cathedral to the river.

View of the West Front of Lincoln Cathedral, from the Castle Hill. This is very similar today, and very popular with today's artists.

Gate Across Bailgate, Lincoln. This is in the Usher Gallery.

Bibliography

Antique Collectors' Club Research Project, *The Royal Watercolour Society, The First Fifty Years 1805-1855,* 1992.

Sir Walter Armstrong, *Memoir of Peter de Wint,* Macmillan, London, 1888.

Harriet De Wint, *A Short Memoir of Peter de Wint and William Hilton, RA,* (unpub).

John Ellis, *A Topographical Landscape by Peter de Wint, OWS* (1784-1849): *The Cultural and Socio-economic Context,* (unpub. pamphlet in Lincoln Central Library).

John Ellis, *Peter de Wint, Walter Christaller and the Carrier's Cart,* (unpub. pamphlet in Lincoln Central Library).

E H Gombrich, *The Story of Art,* Phaidon Press Ltd, Oxford, 14th ed, 1984.

Martin Hardie, *Water-colour Painting in Britain, II The Romantic Period,* B T Batsford, London, 1967.

Charles Holme, ed., *Masters of English Landscape Painting, J.S. Cotman, David Cox and Peter de Wint,* Offices of The Studio, London, 1903.

H W Janson, *A History of Art, A Survey of the Visual Arts from the Dawn of History to the Present Day,* Thames and Hudson, London, 1962.

H L Mallalieu, *The Dictionary of British Watercolour Artists up to 1920, vol II,* Antique Collectors' Club, 1976.

H L Mallalieu, *The Dictionary of British Watercolour Artists up to 1920, vol II: The Plates,* 1979.

H L Mallalieu, *The Dictionary of British Watercolour Artists up to 1920, vol III,* 1990.

Laure Meyer, *Masters of English Landscape,* Pierre Terrait, Paris, 1992.

Gilbert R Redgrave, *The Great Artists, David Cox and Peter de Wint,* Sampson Low, Marston Searle and Rivington, London, 1891.

David Sevase, *Drawings and Watercolours by Peter de Wint,* Cambridge University Press, Cambridge, 1979.

Hammond Smith, *Peter De Wint 1784-1849,* F Lewis, London, 1982.

Stoke on Trent City Museum and Art Gallery, *Peter de Wint 1784-1849, A Bicentenary Exhibition,* 1984.

Basil Taylor, *Stubbs,* Phaidon, London, 1971.

Usher Art Gallery, *Peter de Wint 1784-1849,* 1965.

Usher Art Gallery, *Peter de Wint 1784-1849,* 1998.

Usher Art Gallery, *Frank Bramley RA 1857-1915,* 1999.

Usher Art Gallery, *William Logsdail 1859-1944,* a distinguished painter, 1994.

Usher Art Gallery, *At the Sign of the Dial: Charles Haslewood Shannon and his circle,* 1987.

George C Williamson, ed., *Bryan's Dictionary of Painters and Engravers, vol II,* G Bell and Sons, 1930.

6. 'A Citizen of No Mean City'
Emily Gilbert 1872-1959: Motoring Pioneer and First Woman Sheriff of Lincoln

by Alice Rodgers

IN OLD AGE, EMILY GILBERT was elegant and upright, a dominant presence in any company, yet modest, sweet and smiling with arms outstretched to greet the youngest members of the family. I thought my grandmother's elder sister, Aunt Em, special because of her encyclopaedic knowledge of gardening. She instantly identified plants, flowers and trees and, when I was only seven, taught me the rudiments of pruning. Within the family she was much loved and greatly respected.

Visits to Aunt Em's home, at Sudbrooke, were marked by tours of the neat borders by her house after which my sister and I would be let loose to wander where we would. It was then that, according to season, we would find the platform where the big house had once stood, explore the grass-filled urns of the neglected Italian Garden, make dens among the low-sweeping boughs of the great cedar or venture into the park to forage for nuts and Boy Scout camps. We would return, much later with grubby clothes, to delight Aunt Em with treasures gathered along the way. At the time we didn't regard it as strange that our great aunt had such an enormous garden, that she still drove a car and, at an age when most people were long retired, went to work at Gilbert and Son, Motor Engineers in Lincoln. We also accepted without comment the framed photograph on the wall at home of a, somewhat younger, Emily Gilbert wearing Sheriff's robes. It was not until long after she died that I began to ask questions, to appreciate Emily Gilbert's unique achievements and to admire the determination with which she had pursued her progress from unremarkable origins.

Early life
Emily Gilbert was born on 8 October 1872 at 41 Waterside South, Lincoln, the fourth child and third daughter of William and Fanny Jane Gilbert. William, a blacksmith, had come to Lincoln as a young man in the early 1860s, to seek work first at Clayton and Shuttleworths and later at Robeys. Fanny Jane was ten years his

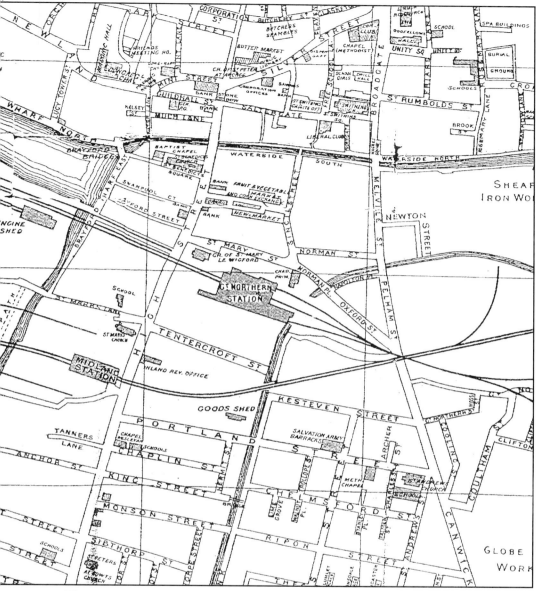

Figure 1. Map showing places mentioned in the text. *Ruddock's Directory of Lincoln, 1903.*

junior, the illegitimate daughter of Jane Wilkinson, whose family hailed from Gainsborough.

Waterside South, at the time of Emily's birth, was a crowded mix of industrial premises, dominated by the Stamp End Works of Clayton and Shuttleworth, and interspersed with rows and courts of workers' housing. Number 41 was in a row situated close to Doughty's Mill on the site later occupied by Rustons. The small, two up two down property was occupied by Emily's parents, her 88 year old great-grandmother, brother Charles and sisters Eleanor and Kate. A younger sister, Jessie, was born in 1874 and a second brother, John, arrived in 1876.

In order to support his rapidly growing family, Emily's father augmented his income by repairing and, later, retailing mangles and sewing machines. In 1876 the family moved to 4, Ripon Street where there was more space for such work which enabled William to leave paid employment and to run his business full time (Figure 1). It was at Ripon Street that Emily acquired another sister, Mary, born in 1879. Two further brothers, James and George and a sister Janetta arrived after the family's move to 28, Melville Street in 1880. Here her father began to make ordinary bicycles (penny farthings).

In the early days of the business, times were hard as the impact of American food imports depressed the agricultural base on which Lincoln's markets, services and engineering industry depended.

Emily's mother was a good manager. She kept the children fed and clad, skilfully nursed them through illnesses and prided herself that none died in infancy. They all went to the Wesleyan School on Rosemary Lane (Figure 2). The children did well and, by 1886, Emily had progressed to Kingsley Street Girls' School, an Anglican foundation in the parish of St Nicholas. It is not clear who first encouraged the talent with figures on which Emily's later livelihood depended but she left school well read, capable at written work and with a thirst for knowledge which never left her.

Lincoln's first woman cyclist?
In the late 1880s, penny farthings gave way to safety bicycles. The former were the province of daring male enthusiasts including Emily's brother Charles. The latter, with chain drive, even-sized wheels and

Figure 2. The façade of the Wesleyan Schools, Rosemary Lane in 2001. *Alice Rodgers.*

Figure 3. The Melville Street premises, c1918, showing bicycles manufactured by Gilbert and Son Ltd. *Gilbert and Son collection.*

pneumatic tyres, were much easier and safer to ride. The bicycling craze burst upon the world and William Gilbert was well placed to prosper from it. Very soon he was producing the Lindum and Royal Lincoln models, fabricating the frames and handlebars but buying in chains, wheels and gears (Figure 3).

There seems no reason to doubt the family tradition that the daredevil teenage Emily, riding one of her father's machines, was the first female cyclist in Lincoln. The story goes that, having been forbidden by William, Emily escaped the house over the back fence, donned her brother's trousers in place of her long skirt and cycled off. When she rode down Carholme Road she was stoned by a group of women who, seeing a woman in trousers dressed like a gold rush camp follower, yelled the insult 'Miss Klondyke'.

As cycling became more respectable, Emily's expertise was put to better use when she was entrusted with the task of teaching various daughters of the Minster Yard how to ride Gilbert machines. It is not known to what extent Emily worked for her father, at this stage, but she certainly acquired sufficient business skills to find employment elsewhere.

Flying the nest

However well William's business succeeded, most of the Gilbert children had to make their own way in the world. On leaving school Charles took up an apprenticeship at Ruston Proctor and Co and began to develop his engineering talent prior to going into partnership with his father. The academically outstanding Eleanor became a teacher and Kate chose nursing as a career. In the early 1890s, Kate moved to a Sheffield hospital to undertake training and with her went Emily, apparently in the hope of training there as well (Figure 4). An independent existence was unthinkable at this time so Emily lodged with her father's Sheffield relatives. She found work in the offices of Vicars and Co, a small manufacturing company.

From this period, a single letter survives, postmarked 16 January 1893 and headed only 'Sheffield'. Written by the twenty year old Emily to her sister Eleanor, then the very lonely and miserable newly appointed headmistress of Long Sutton Board School, it casts light on Emily's activities and attitude to life. Characteristically, Emily's first act was to console her 'darling sister'.

> ...I know how lonely you feel, dearie, it is an old feeling to me now... I only wish I were with you. We could defy all the Long Suttoners and be independent of anyone's friendship but if you get in Lincoln and I get in the Hospital, why we shan't know what ails us, but we shall be as happy as birds on a bough... but we mustn't look for perfect bliss in this world, but be content to get enough to eat and drink with a little happiness thrown in occasionally.

Figure 4. The Gilbert sisters, c1900. Left to right: Janetta, Eleanor, Jessie, Mary, Emily, Kate. *Gilbert and Son collection.*

Elsewhere in the letter Emily writes of her work and demonstrates a mature understanding of business realities.

> *Mr H has not given me a raise as I anticipated, but perhaps he will do later when he has more work, he has nothing in to do. If you see any likelihood of work in this line you might drop me line, with the address of Vicars & Co, he would give me 5% on any work he got...*

Emily also writes of 'the meeting' (perhaps a Sunday school meeting) and reveals, in her account of a conversation with a poor ragged boy, the seeds of what was to become her lifelong Socialism.

> *He finished his pitiful narrative in a whisper 'my big brother has run away and mother says it will break her heart'. Poor little chap. He was no bigger than Janet* [Emily's sister, then aged 6] *and yet he had tasted trouble. The world is indeed sadly out of joint.*

How long Emily remained in Sheffield is not known but by 1898 she had returned to Lincoln to work for her father and brother Charles's business partnership, now incorporated as Gilbert and Son Ltd. Sheffield had made its mark on Emily and she maintained, for the next half century, business contacts established there. Family wedding presents organised by Emily and given jointly with her brother Charles were invariably beautiful canteens of Sheffield cutlery always manufactured by Joseph Elliot and Sons. It seems likely that Emily's Sheffield experience was also influential in Gilbert's decision to diversify into silver plating, an activity for very many years overseen by Jack Panton who hailed from Sheffield.

The first car in Lincoln and the first motorised mail delivery
Gilbert and Son Ltd's *Memorandum and Articles of Association* dated 23 December 1897 show a company poising itself to respond to technological developments. It was to continue as a manufacturer of 'Cycles, Bicycles. Trycycles, Velocipedes and carriages of all kinds', the option to operate in the wider field of mechanical engineering was retained but there was specific provision to deal in 'Carts, Cars, Vehicles, Autocars, Motors and Carriages of all kinds.' The age of motor transport had dawned and, in 1896, it had been Charles Gilbert who drove the first car, a three horsepower Benz (Figure 5) into Lincoln. The year 1899 saw Charles involved in the first use in the provinces by the Royal Mail, of motor transport when he drove the Lincoln assistant postmaster and half a ton of mail in a Daimler Rougemont waggonette to provide a Christmas Day delivery to villages in the fens (Figure 6).

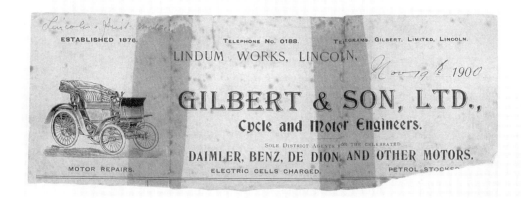

Figure 5. A Gilbert billhead of 1900 showing Lincoln's first car, a three horsepower Benz. *A Rodgers/Gilbert collection.*

In the new company, Emily's book-keeping skills dovetailed well with the inventive engineering expertise of William and Charles. She had a very practical approach to maintaining cash flow in the early days, drawing up invoices quickly and going round on her bicycle delivering them by hand. Only after she had knocked on doors for settlement could the wages be paid. Not everyone responded to her charm but, thanks to her meticulous records, all debts could be pursued. The earliest minute books of the company, which date from 1897, confirm the importance of her work. Emily was trusted and respected by a board of directors composed solely of men. A woman on the board was, at this time, unthinkable.

Figure 6. A Gilbert and Son promotional postcard illustrating the pioneering motorised transport of Christmas Day mails in 1899. Charles Gilbert (driver) and Mr A D Taylor (Assistant Postmaster), are in the Daimler Rougemont waggonette being sent off by Royal Mail staff outside the Sorting Office, Firth Road, Lincoln. *A Rodgers/Gilbert collection.*

Figure 7. Emily Gilbert at the wheel of her car, a Wolseley 14, in c1925.
A Rodgers/Gilbert collection.

Feminist, suffragist and Lincoln's first woman driver

By 1902 Emily's sisters Eleanor and Mary had moved to Kingston upon Thames to take up teaching jobs. Both were concerned at the academic and political inequalities experienced by women and they supported the call for the extension of the franchise. Living close to London they were in a position to watch political developments and to attend suffragist rallies. The Gilbert sisters remained close and the new ideas about votes for women were shared with Emily. For them all, the path towards equality was paved with reasoned argument and by notions of natural justice. Their independence of thought and action in everyday life vouchsafed their beliefs. Before the First World War both Eleanor and Emily had set up their own homes but Emily's most public demonstration of her feminism was to get behind the wheel of a car, probably as early as 1899. She was Lincoln's first woman motorist (Figure 7) and one of the first in the country.

Tents at Skegness and socialist talk

In 1901, Charles Gilbert married a widow, Mary Jane (Polly) Beyan, who brought with her a tent-hire business. The sisters and their mother saw the opportunity to gather together the, now widely dispersed, family and their friends for seaside holidays. Each

Handwritten annotations: *Nellie Jessie Albert Sharp*; *A merry Xmas & good & a good to know & to follow X*; *The man & wife are not members of the family*; *Mary Charlie Mac Jan Fred Castle*

Figure 8. Gilbert family and friends outside a marquee pitched on the North Shore at Skegness in summer 1910. Back row left to right: Eleanor Gilbert, Jessie (Gilbert) Sharp, Albert Sharp. Front row left to right: unknown friend, Mary (Gilbert) Castledine, Charles McSwiggan, unknown friend, Janetta (Gilbert) McSwiggan, William Fred Castledine. *A Rodgers/Gilbert collection.*

summer, thanks largely to Polly and Emily's organisational skills, a well furnished marquee and assorted tents were set up on the North Shore at Skegness provoking a passer-by to describe the Gilberts as 'the gypsies who come here every year' (Figure 8). Following her father's retirement in 1903, Emily was constrained by the needs of the business. Consequently, she came and went to Skegness as she could, bringing supplies of fresh food. Lots of healthy exercise, plenty of reading, watercolour painting and needlecraft were enjoyed but mainly there was the chance to talk, to challenge conventional wisdom and to explore new political ideas. Here, no doubt, plans were made for Emily and Eleanor's trips to the continent in pursuit of art galleries, museums and architecture. Thus Emily's horizons were widened and her cultural and political education were enriched.

Although four of the Gilbert sisters married before 1914, Eleanor and Emily were not among them. According to their youngest sister they did not lack offers but consciously chose career over marriage. Family was, however, of great importance to them and both became the adored aunts of their sisters' children.

The First World War

As for many women of her generation, the First World War offered Emily unexpected opportunities. Her youngest brother, George, who had joined the business following apprenticeship at the Wolsley motor company and a spell managing Wolsley's London office, went off to play his part as a pioneer aviator in the Royal Naval Air Service. Charles, too old to fight, took on war work and, in response to the desperate shortage of agricultural labour, applied his engineering talents to the development of tractor ploughing. This left Emily in day to day charge of a business which included shell case manufacture and the machining of parts for the Foster tanks made in Lincoln.

By 1916 Emily had become a shareholder and attended annual meetings of the company. In 1919, she and George were made directors and on the 21 November 1919 Emily was voted a bonus of £100 for her work during the war. At this time she was, effectively, in sole management of the business as Charles Gilbert was in charge of the Food Production Department. Better still they appointed her Company Secretary.

The inter-war period

Between 1919 and 1939 cars ceased to be rich men's toys and, with volume production and increased reliability, became more common. Gilbert and Son adapted to meet new needs. Its growing agricultural business was focussed on new premises in Bourne and cars and commercial vehicles became central to the Lincoln undertaking. Manufacture and sales of cycles continued as did the silver plating business. A wholesale company was developed and, at Emily's instigation, a hire purchase company was set up.

Despite the difficulties of the period, the business was usually profitable. Charles's salary reflected his additional management responsibilities but, as directors in 1920, Emily and George were well and, more to the point, equally paid.

In 1920 the registered office of the company was moved to premises purchased on Pelham Street and, about this time, a large flat was created for Emily over the cycle shop in Oxford Street. Emily owned a car and took holidays abroad but her lifestyle hardly reflected her income.

It was in her nature to invest wisely and, even before the First World War, she had personally acquired property in locations which might later be useful to the company.

The extended family

Living in the town centre Emily's only unmet desire was to have a garden. By 1921, clearly wishing to revive the family holidays among the dunes at Skegness, she had purchased a rather primitive seaside bungalow at Landseer Avenue, Chapel St Leonards. Travelling by train and cycle, it was to make her garden at Chapel that she escaped when she could. Each summer her sisters' families gathered there for holidays which featured bracing walks, cold sea bathing and ginger cake (Figure 9).

Family continued to be enormously important and Emily travelled to Dublin each Christmas to be with her sister Janetta and her children. By them, she is remembered as a fairy godmother, always arriving with lots of little gifts and treats. In 1932, on one of Jan's children's visits to Lincolnshire, they were delighted to be accommodated in a real gypsy caravan and a tent set up amongst the dunes at Chapel. Emily never lost either her touch with children or her love of the Lincolnshire coast. The high spot of our family's

Figure 9. Family and friends in the garden of Emily Gilbert's bungalow at Chapel St Leonards, August 1921. Back row left to right: Sam Freshney, Charles Gilbert, unknown female holding Martin Castledine, Freshney son. On Chairs left to right: Emily Gilbert, Maud Hindle, Mrs Freshney, Mary Castledine, Polly Gilbert. Kneeling left to right: Peg Goss, Elizabeth Castledine, Gilbert Sharp. Cross-legged left to right: Christopher Castledine, Freshney daughter, Louis Goss. *A Rodgers/Gilbert collection.*

holiday at Sudbrooke, in 1952, was when Aunt Em entrusted my father to drive us, in her new Morris Oxford, for a day trip and picnic at Chapel. Emily also remembered the family when debts were paid. Amongst her customers, in the early 1930s, was an excellent tailor who was persuaded to settle, in kind, a long overdue bill. Honour was satisfied, the company reimbursed and my father and his cousin were sent to be fitted for dress suits.

The Sudbrooke years

Following her sister Eleanor's retirement, in 1925, Emily looked for a new home which they could share. In about 1928 she purchased Sudbrooke Park where the pair eventually set up home at Garden House. This, with its conservatory and large grounds, offered enormous scope for Emily's horticultural talents. She also ran a market garden at Sudbrooke.

By now Emily was well known in Lincoln through her work in the business and because of involvement with local activities. Although Charles became a Conservative member of the Council, Emily remained socialist in outlook. She took particular interest in staff welfare, in the training of company apprentices and she encouraged employees to take their bonuses as company shares. Gilberts could never be a workers' co-operative but, under Emily's influence, the staff was both loyal and long-serving.

First woman sheriff of Lincoln

In 1936, at the age of 64, Emily was invited by the Labour Mayor elect, Councillor J E Fordham, to serve as City Sheriff (Figure 10). In his speech on Monday 9 November proposing her appointment Councillor J K Fox made much of the novelty that Emily Gilbert, the 936th Sheriff, was to be the first woman ever to hold office. The councillors who proposed her made no bones about the risk they were taking but drew attention to the part Miss Gilbert had played in obtaining the franchise for women. 'In these days of science and industry there is scarcely anything we can say is only a man's job.'

Emily responded with characteristic vigour and with delicious irony quoted, the supreme misogynist, Paul of Tarsus.

Figure 10. Official portrait of Emily Gilbert, Sheriff of Lincoln, 1936-37.
A Rodgers/Gilbert Collection

Throughout the years, women have been regarded as anything from chattels to angels but this honour, paid to a woman, is a recognition of the admission of women to full citizenship. With St Paul I can say that 'I am a citizen of no mean city'.

Emily made a gracious and good sheriff and enjoyed her public duties which she carried out mostly unsupported by a Sheriff's Lady. Her appointment had come as the Abdication Crisis reached its height and a month later Emily was in the Minster Yard for the proclamation of the new King, George VI. She was still in office at the time of his Coronation on 13 May 1937 and features in Lincoln's official publication to mark the event.

In September 1937, along with the nineteen other Sheriffs of the Counties Corporate in England and Wales, Emily attended celebrations in Exeter to mark the four hundredth anniversary of that city's shrievalty. To the sheriffs of Lincoln and of Berwick upon Tweed fell the honour of replying to the toast to the guests.

Emily's correspondence with the town clerk of Exeter shows her desire not to allow the robing room to remain a male preserve. The Town Clerk advised that the lady sheriff of Worcester would be processing to and from the cathedral in court dress without a robe, involving her in two substantial changes of clothing. There was, he said, no room in the Guildhall for the women to robe separately. Emily replied

... in my case I wear the official robe, chain and hat so there is no difficulty about robing in a separate room since these are, of course put on over my other wearing apparel.

Exeter Corporation had chartered an eight-seater DH Dragon plane to take three of the sheriffs, including Emily, to the event. Special permission was obtained to fly from RAF Waddington via Rochester and Southampton but fog grounded the aircraft. A car was hastily arranged to take Emily and her sister Mary Castledine, her escort for the occasion, to a rendezvous near London with under sheriff Sir Charles and Lady McRae. Shortly afterwards, the vehicle broke down. Somehow the party got to Paddington and, fortified by a slap-up meal at the *Great Western Hotel*, proceeded by rail. In a letter to Emily, Sir Charles later described it as 'a bit of an adventure' and their journey became the talk of the civic dinner they missed at Exeter Guildhall. Despite the smoothness of the return flight, the story still hit the newspapers. Exeter Corporation insisted on reimbursing all expenses including the meal!

According to her sisters, as sheriff, the only duty which Emily dreaded was the need to witness executions at Lincoln Prison. Fortunately none took place during her term. In November 1937, in yet another first for the Gilberts, Emily was succeeded by her brother Charles. He and Polly revived the Sheriff's Garden Party which was held at Sudbrooke with Emily, now High Constable, in the receiving line. It is some indication of the extent to which Emily was ahead of her time that 50 years were to pass before there was a second woman Sheriff. Only Norah Baldock (1986) and Irene Goldson (1994) have yet followed in her footsteps.

The Second World War.

Charles Gilbert died in 1939 and, shortly after, George went off to a distinguished service career in REME. Once more Emily was alone at the helm as the works was adapted for military training purposes. She was ably supported by Ernest Radford, works manager, a longstanding and close family friend who had been made a director. The worst moment of Emily's war came, in July 1941, when two RAF planes collided above the Oxford Street premises killing Ernest (Figure 11). Emily, nearing her 70s, strove on with the support of Hilda Menzies, a long-serving employee who became company secretary in February 1942.

Figure 11. Press report of the air crash over Oxford Street, July 1941. *Gilbert and Son collection.*

116   SATURDAY, 2 AUGUST, 1941

Planes Collide In Mid-Air.

Three Killed Nine Injured

...achines Crash on Lincoln Houses

...ILOTS SAVED BY PARACHUTES

After colliding in mid-air near Lincoln on Sunday evening two R.A.F. 'planes crashed on houses in different parts of the city, killing three people and injuring nine others.

Many people witnessed

The post-war period and Pelham Bridge

After the war, George returned as managing director but died in 1947. Thus, at the age of 75, Emily became managing director. In 1949 Gilberts altered its rules to permit directors to serve beyond the age of 70 and Emily continued in office. Wartime restrictions and shortages of materials made the post-war period one of particular difficulty for the motor trade. In the early 1950s new models began to appear and people accepted a long wait for cars. It was with glee that Aunt Em telephoned in 1953 to say she had found a 1952 model Morris Minor for my father.

The mid-1950s was the time of greatest challenge. The construction of Pelham Bridge was in prospect and that would mean the demolition of the company premises. Emily, now in her 80s, was not superhuman. She was troubled by cataracts and relied to an increasing degree on others. Hilda Menzies was depended upon at the works, the loyal and devoted Sam Snell drove her on anything other than local journeys and her niece, Fan Goss, kept house. Her nephews Martin Castledine and, later, Niall McSwiggan joined the company. At first Niall and his wife lived in Sudbrooke Park where they observed Emily, determined to the last, cycling with a hoe over her shoulder, to tend distant parts of her garden (Figure 12).

Emily continued active in local life. She was a Soroptomist, a founder member of the Lincoln branch of the National Council of Women and a member of the United Nations Association, Lincoln Automobile Association and Lincoln Civic Trust. Sudbrooke Park was used for camps by Lincoln and District Boy Scouts of which she was a Vice President, and shortly before her death she gave six acres there for a permanent scout campsite.

Emily lived to see the demolition of Gilbert's works, the move to temporary premises in Norman Street and the opening of Pelham Bridge in June 1958. During the last year of her life she was ill and burdened by

Figure 12. Emily Gilbert, octogenarian gardener, in her conservatory at Sudbrooke, c1958. *Gilbert and Son collection.*

negotiations over the siting and building of new premises for Gilberts. On 25 May 1959 she attended her last director's meeting, held at Sudbrooke, which made provision for a new director, from outside the family, to take over her work. A fortnight later, aged 86, Emily died of cancer.

It was an enormous funeral at St Andrew's Church attended by her large family, staff and former staff, civic dignitaries, representatives of industry and commerce in Lincoln, of the motor industry nationally and of the organisations she had supported. All were proud to be numbered among the friends of Emily Gilbert, a woman of dignity and integrity and an outstanding citizen of Lincoln.

Notes and References

This article is based upon an inherited collection of material about the Gilbert family which came to me on the death of my father, Christopher Castledine. This includes the family Bible started by William and Fanny Jane Gilbert, Emily Gilbert's file of memorabilia relating to her term as Sheriff, letters, press cuttings, certificates, wills, estate accounts and family photographs as well as my father's meticulously referenced notes on the history of Gilbert and Son Ltd. In celebration of the company's centenary in 1976, my father's cousins, Niall and Philip McSwiggan prepared a tape/slide talk and an album of copies of old photographs. These materials, together with minute books and newspaper cuttings in the Gilbert and Son deposit in Lincolnshire Archives, have cast additional light on Emily Gilbert's life.

Acknowledgements

I owe a debt of gratitude to the members of the Gilbert family including my great-grandmother (Fanny Jane Gilbert), her daughters (Eleanor and Emily Gilbert, Mary Castledine and Janetta McSwiggan) and her grandchildren (Christopher Castledine and Niall McSwiggan) who have written things down, related and retold family stories and preserved records of the family and the company. In the preparation of this article I have received help from various members of the family including my sister Ruth Saunders, my cousins David Castledine and Maurice Rahman and my father's cousin Moira Starkey. I am particularly grateful for Niall McSwiggan's advice and constructive comments on the text. Thanks are also due to James Stevenson of Lincolnshire Archives for guidance regarding the Gilbert papers, to Mrs Julie N Duxbury (Civic Manager, Lincoln City Council) for a prompt reply to a detailed letter about former Sheriffs of Lincoln and to Brian Elliott for help with illustrations.

7. THE MIDDLE CLASSES IN VICTORIAN LINCOLN

by Kate Hill

IN THE NINETEENTH CENTURY, and particularly between 1850 and 1900, Lincoln changed enormously; and one of the most significant transformations was in its social composition. The rise of the huge engineering companies stimulated population growth, and their large workforces brought terraced housing development and a different type of employee/employer relationship from that of the small workshop firm.[1] At the same time, the influence of the county's great landed families slowly started to wane within the city.[2] But what of the middling ranks, those who were neither 'county families', nor manual workers, but used capital, or professional knowledge, or trade to make a living? This chapter will investigate the effect that Lincoln's development had on them, and also, equally important, the effect that they had on Lincoln's development.

Lincoln, in bringing together some of the characteristics of both the county market town, and the industrial, rapidly growing town, may allow further light to be shed on the Victorian middle classes nationally. Much of the work that has been done on the Victorian middle classes has focussed on industrial cities like Manchester and Leeds, and has looked at the problems faced by them in tackling public health problems, unruly streets, challenges to their authority, and labour unrest. In addition, the extremely divided nature of the middle classes, in terms of religion, politics and interests, has been noted; measures were taken to overcome this, by creating clubs and societies where divisions meant less than common interests.[3] Significantly, the emergence of a clear middle class was coterminous with the emergence of residential segregation in these cities; those who could afford to move out of the increasingly crowded and polluted centre did so, forming middle-class suburbs ever more leafy, exclusive and distant from working-class areas.[4]

However, those cities, though important and populous, were relatively few in number, and much less work has been done on smaller, less industrial towns. In such towns, there may have been less need to 'improve' the working class and to legitimate middle-class authority, as urban problems and industrial relations may have been less severe, while traditional social patterns persisted. Residential segregation by class has been supposed to be much less advanced in smaller towns than large, wealthy manufacturing towns.

In the eighteenth and early nineteenth centuries, an ill-defined precursor to the middle-class emerged, the 'middling sort', a widely varying group comprising master craftsmen, tenant farmers, merchants and dealers, and professionals, mainly lawyers, doctors and clergy.[5] At some point from the beginning of the nineteenth century, this pattern shifted to produce a more recognisably modern middle-class; for many, the place of work became separate from the home. The home became a place for the family alone, so apprentices and work employees were much less likely to live-in (though domestic servants, of course, increased). In families that considered themselves middle class, women wherever possible withdrew completely from involvement in the business, and restricted themselves to domestic management and charitable work.[6] So the development of a 'modern' rather than 'traditional' middle class was not just about the way they dominated and shaped the urban environment, it was also about new ideas on the proper roles and relationships of men and women, the family, and the workplace. However, again this process has been most clearly documented in large towns and cities, such as Birmingham. An examination of the Lincoln middle classes, then, should allow us to see how widespread the development of a new middle class was in the nineteenth century, as well as shedding some light on Lincoln's own history.

This chapter will briefly outline economic, political, social and cultural changes among Lincoln's middle classes, and will suggest that despite the impact of a few large industrialists, middle-class development was not as dramatic as comparisons with large industrial towns would suggest.

In the first half of the nineteenth century, Lincoln's middle class has been seen as part of a 'traditional urban culture', made up of an elite of bankers, professional men, resident gentry and families of independent means, with a lower stratum consisting of shopkeepers and tradesmen, either providing goods and services for the elite, or processing agricultural produce. Thus the county town middle class is argued to have been both larger and more characterised by 'traditional' relationships of service and deference than its counterpart in fast-expanding manufacturing towns. The impetus for change among the middle class of county towns such as Northampton was the changing scale and organisation of manufacturing, which increased conflict between employers and employees, increased middle class wealth, and made town centres less pleasant places, thereby stimulating the growth of middle class suburbs.[7] How far, then, was Lincoln's economy transformed in a similar fashion?

Economic change and the middle class

Lincoln of course started the century with an economy and population damaged by centuries of decline. However, revival had begun strongly in the eighteenth century, as transport improved.[8] Growth areas were not, before 1850, particularly industrial; the shock industries of the industrial revolution, textiles, mining or iron smelting, were not represented. Rather they were small-scale, with low levels of mechanisation, and were aimed at servicing the agricultural lands around Lincoln. Thus milling both for oil and corn, producing animal feeds as well as flour, was prominent, and by the 1830s was starting to utilise steam as well as wind; and steam packet owners based around Brayford Pool prospered in the years before the arrival of the railways.[9] Malting and brewing, always found on a small scale in market towns, expanded into regional or national businesses. None of these types of enterprise were very large employers, though most of them would have had some employees. Their importance lies both in the reasonably solid base of middling income they produced, and in the build up of some technical knowledge about steam engines and modern machinery, which was crucial to the next phase of Lincoln's development. In addition, as a market and county town in a predominantly rural area, with a cathedral and its concomitant body of clergy, Lincoln had a fairly large proportion of professionals, shopkeepers, and various other middle class occupations which serviced the rural population.

In 1856, which may be considered the brink of Lincoln's industrial expansion, the number of those entitled to vote in parliamentary elections, which at the time was a reasonable marker of 'middle classness', was 1,349, This is roughly 31 per cent of the adult male population. The number of municipal voters was 2,261, about 52 per cent.[10] These figures are fairly high for the time, and certainly higher than in towns which had industrialised and expanded faster than Lincoln; these tended to have numbers of parliamentary voters forming only ten to eighteen per cent of the adult male population.[11] One reason for this apparently large middle class is that the freemen voters included many working men, so the figure needs to be revised downwards to some degree. Nevertheless, a picture emerges which confirms that Lincoln had a generally traditional, county town middle class in the first half of the nineteenth century.

In the 1850s, a series of engineering firms, producing portable steam engines, threshing machines, and similar items for a predominantly agricultural market, developed in Lincoln.[12] Their rise was dramatic and fast, and they soon became classic industrial units, employing thousands, and bringing spectacular, new wealth to their owners.[13] These men came from typical middling backgrounds: Clayton and Shuttleworth were a steam packet owner and a small shipbuilder respectively, and Ruston came from a farming background and was apprenticed as a cutler in Sheffield.[14] Theirs was not a 'rags to riches' story, but one of a transition from moderate income to riches. Nevertheless, they were not from the landed or 'county' families, and their use of their new wealth, leisure and position was distinctive. It also seems that they developed new types of relations with their increasingly large numbers of employees.

However, there were few of this new breed of industrialist, though their significance was out of proportion to their numbers. Most of the middle class were still small employers if at all, working in partnerships or individually. Growth in population and wealth, however, affected many, in less spectacular fashion. In this Lincoln follows the national trend. The leading group within Lincoln's middle class had always been its professionals; there were a large number of high-ranking clergy in Lincoln, of course, and doctors and lawyers, coming from families that could afford expensive and prolonged educations, aligned themselves with the landed interest rather than the tradesmen of the city. However, after 1850, the ranks of the professions swelled in Lincoln as elsewhere; not only were there more of the traditional professions, but they were joined by new occupations such as architects and accountants. By 1892, 23 doctors and 32 lawyers were listed in *Kelly's Directory*, but there were also two naturalists, five dentists, two librarians and two veterinary surgeons, as well as a greatly expanded range of jobs in local government. Few of these had quite the prestige of the older professions; something like teaching covered a broad status range, and teachers at elementary schools could claim very little in the way of salary or status.

Commerce and small-scale production continued to be very important in terms of numbers of people involved, and also profited from population growth. Milling and selling corn, animal feed and similar products were strong throughout the period. Builders and developers did well, as they did nationally, and one of the largest employers in 1851 was a builder employing 125.[15] Merchants and shopkeepers were numerous and prosperous. Again, by 1892 we see an extremely broad range of merchants, dealers and shopkeepers, and though some would undoubtedly have been single-handed, small enterprises keeping their owner's head above water, the 50 or so merchants based at the Corn Exchange, the ten wine and spirit merchants, and various substantial timber and coal merchants would have been very comfortable; William Spencer, a timber merchant, living in Tentercroft Street in 1881, employed two domestic servants. Lincoln supported a piano dealer and a curiosity dealer.[16]

So in the second half of the nineteenth century, the initial image is one of almost a boom town, certainly for the middle classes. This period coincides too with the arrival of the railways in Lincoln, an event which stimulated the economy in many ways, facilitating the transport of coal and other raw materials to Lincoln, and of manufactured and agricultural products away. It also brought large numbers of workers, over a period of years, who spent money in Lincoln. However, the nineteenth century economy was quite savagely cyclical, and Lincoln was not immune. In the 1880s a deep depression hit the city, affecting several sectors. The big industrial firms were badly hit, although they had recovered by the end of the century; they had to resort to laying off workers and wage cuts.[17] This brought resistance among the workers, who as skilled workers already had a high level of unionisation. Industrial action, with varying degrees of success, followed. Though trade revived, by 1892 the Lincoln Trades and Labour Council had been formed.[18] Thus the manufacturers had to deal with organised, more powerful employees, as textile mill owners and other industrialists in Britain had already had to. However, as we have seen, these were only a few individuals; most of the Lincoln middle class dealt with only a few of the working class at a time, as employees and servants, or maybe as co-religionists. General labourers had great difficulty even in forming a union.[19] The majority of the middle class were not, therefore, particularly concerned with the growing strength of organised labour and its demands for shorter working hours, better wages, and better working conditions.

Local government
However, the Lincoln middle classes did have to address some of the same problems as their equivalents in cities such as Manchester, Sheffield and Birmingham: public health, public order and public amenities. Lincoln's fastest growth came relatively late, at a time when many cities were taking steps to remedy these problems. What

was the nature of the middle classes' involvement in Lincoln local government, as a major means of tackling these problems? While the selection of MPs remained largely influenced by the landed interest until the last quarter of the nineteenth century, the city council was a different affair. Its composition over time is hard to analyse effectively because of the relatively small numbers involved (there was a total of 24 in the council), but it seems that over the second half of the nineteenth century, the proportion of professionals and industrialists went down, while that of shopkeepers, traders and small manufacturers went up. Between the 1850s and 1870s, Clayton, Shuttleworth, Penistan and Ruston all served on the council; there were no manufacturers on the council in 1892. Professionals such as Dr Swan and Dr R S Harvey were leading figures on the council in the 1850s. This trend in council membership, tentatively identified though it is, may help to explain the notorious inactivity of Lincoln city council. It engaged in the absolute minimum of measures to safeguard public order, and in terms of public health and amenities was even more dilatory. Of course, in the nineteenth century, it was a firmly held tenet that government, local or national, should do as little as possible, but from 1850, city councils elsewhere were increasingly not just doing the minimum to preserve order and alleviate disease a little, but were actively undertaking projects to improve the appearance of their cities, setting up libraries, art galleries and museums, building public baths and opening parks, with a positive zeal in some places. In Lincoln, by contrast, even a decent sewage system had to wait until the council was threatened by central government, and work was not started till 1876.[20]

There are of course a number of reasons for this. Lincoln, though growing, and with a reasonable revenue from property rents, was still much smaller than any of the great Victorian cities, and therefore its council had much less money to spend. However, this natural disadvantage was compounded by the council's refusal to set a borough rate until 1874, though parish and later urban sanitary authority rates were levied.[21] Without any rates coming in, the council could not afford to take any great initiatives. Another contrast between Lincoln's council and that of, say Birmingham, is that during the period when Birmingham's council was undertaking bold projects, it was made up of many of the city's leading citizens – wealthy manufacturers, prominent professionals – and was very strongly supported by others, such as leading clergymen and yet more wealthy manufacturers. Many of these people were linked through their membership of a small number of Nonconformist chapels, especially Unitarian, Congregational and Quaker.[22] Many councils went through a period when 'economist' or 'ratepayer' groups, usually lower middle class or even upper working class, hard hit by rate increases, challenged municipal spending and scuppered more grandiose projects; however, these challenges were usually seen off by wealthier councillors.[23]

In Lincoln, by contrast, as we have seen, there were at best only ever a few leading citizens on the council, and their influence waned as the Victorian period progressed. There was little of the 'old' Nonconformity, Quakerism, Unitarianism and Congregationalism, which stressed civic service, in Lincoln; Methodism was very healthy, but does not at this stage appear to have particularly encouraged its members into local government.[24] For those who formed the majority of Lincoln's council, there was little to be gained from expanding its responsibilities; they were not large-scale employers, and faced only a small amount of drunkenness and prostitution on the streets in comparison with a large city; and there were already a reasonable number of amenities available on a commercial basis for the middle classes. On the other hand, as small-scale businessmen, the imposition of a rate would hurt them much more than it would the very rich; although as a sector trade and small manufacturing was healthy, individuals were quite insecure and bankruptcy never far away. Hostility to rates and council expenditure, which was strong enough to lead to death threats to councillors, was attributed at the time to small landlords, who owned modest numbers of working-class houses, sometimes effectively as pensions; the possible impact on this group of rate rises is obvious.[25]

Residential patterns and domestic ideology

How far was Lincoln's middle class becoming a distinctive group in terms of its residential patterns and domestic ideology?[26] Although there is no room here for a thorough investigation, it seems to be the case that Lincoln's middle class was slower to adopt new patterns of living than historians would expect. In the 1881 census, many tradesmen, small manufacturers and shopkeepers seem to conform to an allegedly earlier pattern of middle class life. William Wilcox, a chemist living in Guildhall Street, employed an assistant, an apprentice, and a servant (presumably domestic), all of whom lived-in. Marianne Stainton, who kept a bookshop, also of Guildhall Street, had two employees and one servant, again all living-in. Both also lived at their place of work. Now of course, it is clear that shopkeepers and tradesmen were particularly slow to adopt habits of excluding employees from the home (other than servants), and moving away from their place of work, because of the very nature of that work. It is also clear that in other strata of the middle class, these patterns had emerged. For example, in 1881, Robert Swan, a prominent solicitor, lived at 'The Quarries', out of the built-up area on Greetwell Road, with his wife, seven children and nine domestic servants. However, although there were significant examples of such lifestyles, they were by no means a characteristic of the middle class as a whole. These examples also indicate the gulf in wealth and status among the middle class; the houses of men such as Robert Swan, and the judge James Stephen who lived in Newport House with five servants, stood out in whatever part of Lincoln they were situated. The large engineering manufacturers, similarly, lived away from their

Figure 1. Eastgate house, the home of Alfred Shuttleworth. *From the Local Studies Collection, Lincoln Central Library, by courtesy of Lincolnshire County Council, Education and Cultural Services Directorate.*

Figure 2. Monks Manor, the home of Joseph Ruston. *From the Local Studies Collection, Lincoln Central Library, by courtesy of Lincolnshire County Council, Education and Cultural Services Directorate.*

Figure 3. An interior view of Monks Manor: the picture gallery. *From the Local Studies Collection, Lincoln Central Library, by courtesy of Lincolnshire County Council, Education and Cultural Services Directorate.*

factories in some splendour. At this point they lived close to the cathedral, in the area where formerly county families had kept a town house.[27] Ruston lived in Monks Manor, with his wife and seven children, and seven live-in servants, as well as gardeners, grooms and coachmen, while Alfred Shuttleworth lived in Eastgate House with five servants, and Nathaniel Clayton lived in Eastcliffe House with four servants and a coachman (see Figures 1-3). Later both Shuttleworth and Clayton bought houses outside Lincoln.

However, there are some signs of more conventional residential segregation in Lincoln if we examine the evidence of the 1881 census; a road such as Tentercroft Street had a modest middle class occupancy, with household heads' occupation ranging from blacksmith at the bottom, to solicitors, architects and doctors at the top, with a large number of annuitants and retired tradesmen in the middle. Significantly, households in Tentercroft Street in 1881 had an average of 1.2 servants, and none contained live-in employees other than servants. Lindum Road contained ten households, with an average of 2.2 domestic servants. Occupations of the head of household included draper, solicitor, painter and retired people. Significantly, both here and on Monks Road, with an average of just under one servant per household, women, generally widows, were a notable proportion of heads of household: 22 per cent for Monks Road, and 40 per cent for Lindum Road in 1881. Some of these women are listed as having boarders, but some clearly also had independent incomes, such as Charlotte Norton who lived on Lindum Road with a companion and two servants. This is an important fact to bear in mind when examining the occupational and civic characteristics of the middle class. Clear high status areas were emerging, such as Greetwell Road, and Lindum Terrace, with averages of nearly 3.5, and 2.5 servants per household respectively in 1881.[28]

The development of class identity
It is clear, therefore, that the Lincoln middle class in the second half of the nineteenth century was a disparate, not to say divided, group. There were wide variations in income, standard of living, residential pattern, and approach to local government. To a certain extent, an elite, consisting of lawyers, some doctors, and a few industrialists, had separated out from the rest, and was marked by residence above hill, close to the cathedral, maybe in a large new house with plenty of servants, and with a 'progressive' attitude to local government. To what extent was this pattern reinforced by the creation of cultural institutions?

There was already a group of elite institutions stemming from an earlier period, such as the assembly rooms dating from the eighteenth century. These were joined by new ones such as the Permanent Subscription Library, established in 1814, with a subscription of one guinea; the Lincoln Library, which was actually a kind of literary society, in existence from 1814 to 1909; the Temple Gardens, which closed in 1863, with a yearly subscription of 20s., and various subscription concerts and short-lived musical societies, about whose social make-up we know little, such as the Choral Society founded in 1856. In addition, in 1873 the Lincoln Club was revived, forming an exclusive venue for the men of the top ranks of professions, manufacture and trade, as well as clergymen and gentry.[29]

Charitable institutions have also been seen as an important cultural tool for creating a distinctive middle class, and in Lincoln it is certainly possible that they acted to integrate the newly forming elite, comprising more traditionally high status groups as well as the newly rich. For example, the Lincoln School of Science and Art was fostered by a combination of the leading clergy, along with other professionals and the leading industrialists, and was supported by a broad range of Lincoln society.[30]

However, objects of charity were fairly traditional in Lincoln, with health and the relief of poverty through, for example, soup kitchens, forming the bulk of initiatives.[31] Education, in the shape of the Mechanics Institute from the first half of the century, and the Lincoln School of Science and Art in the second, was also a focus which one would expect from a town with a high proportion of clergy.

Conclusion

Trends and patterns can only be identified very tentatively on the basis of this brief overview. Nevertheless, it seems clear that the impact of the large industrialists was limited. They took part in local government in the third quarter of the nineteenth century, presumably motivated at least partly by their employment of large numbers of working men; it was an opportunity to improve their employees' living conditions, and enhance their own authority.[32] However, local government was particularly sluggish and resistant to innovation in Lincoln, and the large industrialists seem to have retreated from the council, moving into more prestigious public roles as MPs and JPs. At the same time, they grew closer to the old elite in philanthropic activities such as soup kitchens, and on a different level, the School of Science and Art, as well as in residential patterns.[33] Meanwhile the rest of Lincoln's middle class very reluctantly undertook minimal public health improvements, very little civic improvement, and largely maintained the social and cultural institutions of 1800. Although expanded and diversified, it was still a class dominated by the service needs of a county and market town, and its members lived in very similar ways to an earlier middle class. It did have a broader and richer range of professionals, merchants and retired people who adopted a new, pseudo-suburban way of life complete with villas and batteries of domestic servants; but overall, despite Lincoln's increasingly modern economy, its middle class was much more traditional than studies of larger cities would suggest.

Notes and References

1. Population growth started before the birth of the big engineering firms, with a modest but steady growth throughout the eighteenth century. However, the high growth rates in the second half of the nineteenth century, reaching nearly 40 per cent between 1871 and 1881, may be at least partly attributed to the large numbers employed in those firms. Sir Francis Hill, *Victorian Lincoln*, Cambridge University Press 1974, appendix 1.

2. F Hill, *Victorian Lincoln*, p.304.

3. See for example R J Morris, *Class Sect and Party, The Making of the British Middle Class: Leeds 1820-1850*, Manchester University Press 1990; J Wolff and John Seed, eds., *The Culture of Capital: Art, Power and the Nineteenth Century Middle Class*, Manchester University Press 1988; A J Kidd and K W Roberts, eds., *City, Class and Culture: Studies of Social Policy and Cultural Production in Victorian Manchester*, Manchester University Press 1985; Kidd and Nicholls, eds., *Gender, Civic Culture and Consumerism: Middle Class Identity in Britain 1800-1940*, Manchester University Press 1999.

4. F M L Thompson, 'Town and City', in F M L Thompson, ed., *The Cambridge Social History of Britain 1750-1950, vol. 1: Regions and Communities*, Cambridge University Press 1990, pp.60-62.

5. J Smail, *The Origins of Middle Class Culture: Halifax, Yorkshire, 1660-1780*, Ithaca. N.Y.: Cornell University Press 1994; John Seed, 'From 'middling sort' to middle class in late eighteenth and early nineteenth century England', in M L Bush, ed., *Social Orders and Social Classes in Europe since 1500: Studies in Social Stratification*, Harlow: Longman 1992 .

6. Leonora Davidoff and Catherine Hall, *Family Fortunes, Men and Women of the English Middle-Class*, 1780-1850, Routledge: London 1992.

7. R J Morris, 'The middle class and British towns and cities of the Industrial Revolution, 1780-1870', in D Fraser and A Sutcliffe, ed., *The Pursuit of Urban History*, London: Edward Arnold 1983, pp.289-290.

8. Peter Borsay, *The English Urban Renaissance: Culture and Society in the Provincial Town*, 1660-1770, Oxford: Clarendon 1991, p.23.

9. F Hill, *Victorian Lincoln*, p.99-100.

10. *White's Directory of Lincolnshire*, 1856. Following Richard H Trainor, *Black Country Elites: The Exercise of Authority in an Industrialised Area 1830-1900*, Oxford University Press 1993, p.63, I have taken the adult male population to be one quarter of the total population.

11. Trainor, *Black Country Elites*, p.63.

12. Clayton and Shuttleworth set up their firm in 1842; Robey and Co. was founded in 1854; Foster's switched from flour milling to machine making in 1856; and Ruston joined Burton and Proctor, later to become Ruston, Proctor and Co., in 1857. Hill pp.120-123.

13. Clayton and Shuttleworth employed 1,200 by 1870; Ruston, Proctor and Co. 1,600 by 1889; Hill pp.122, 202.

14. Hill p.123.

15. He was Charles Ward, who served on the council, and was later Mayor. Hill p.124.

16. *Kelly's Directory of Lincolnshire* 1892.

17. Hill p.207.

18. Hill p.209.

19. Hill p.208.

20. Hill p.170.

21. Hill p.230.

22. E P Hennock, *Fit and Proper Persons: Ideal and Reality in Nineteenth Century Urban Government*, London: Edward Arnold 1973; R Hartnell, 'Art and Civic Culture in Birmingham in the Late Nineteenth Century', *Urban History* 22, 2 (1995)

23. Trainor, *Black Country Elites*, p.255.

24. For details of churches and chapels, see the various directories for these years.

25. Hill p.166-7.

26. By 1894, residential segregation in Lincoln as a whole was not especially marked; Mills and Edgar found a pattern of mid-status housing on street fronts, with low-status in the courts behind. This kind of pattern can be found in many Victorian towns, and indeed earlier as well. However, they suggest a stronger clustering of the elite 'above hill'; this again would be consistent with findings such as Mills' that the group showing strongest segregation in the Victorian town was the upper middle-class. Dennis Mills and Michael Edgar, 'Social history in Lincoln's Victorian residential streets', *Local Population Studies Society Newsletter 27*, September 2000, pp. 4-10; Richard Dennis, *English Industrial Cities of the Nineteenth Century*, Cambridge University Press 1984.

27. Hill, p.63.

28. Lincoln Census 1881 - CEBs RG11/3240, RG11/3243.

29. *White's Directory of Lincolnshire*, 1856; Hill, p.150, p. 222; *Kelly's Directory of Lincolnshire* 1885.

30. Unpublished paper by Dennis Mills, 'The Lincoln School of Science and Art'; for a full listing of those who subscribed to or sat on the committee of the School, see D and J Mills, 'The New Lincoln School of Science and Art, who built it and who paid for it?', Lincoln Central Library, unbound pamphlets UP12811.

31. *White's Directory of Lincolnshire* 1856.

32. Ruston and Proctor urged action on working-class housing in Lincoln on behalf of their workpeople in the early twentieth century; Hill, *Victorian Lincoln*, p.291

33. Hill, p.297.

8. THOMAS WATSON: THE LAST ROMAN CATHOLIC BISHOP OF LINCOLN

by John Wilford

NO SINGLE FIGURE IN LINCOLN'S HISTORY better illustrates the Reformation from a Catholic perspective than Bishop Thomas Watson (Figure 1). He lived through it and describes it vividly as a tragedy – as calamitous as any classical Greek or Roman Tragedy, or any tragedy found in the Scriptures.

When Watson was born, near Durham in 1515, Cardinal Wolsey was Henry VIII's Lord Chancellor and the Pope's Legate. He governed state and church. England was arguably the most Catholic country in Christendom. Henry received three 'Golden Rose' awards from three popes. These were presented to monarchs and rulers 'conspicuous for their Catholic spirit and loyalty to the Holy See, and as a mark of esteem and personal affection'.[1] When Luther attacked the Pope and the Church, Henry VIII leapt to their defence. Watson was six years old when Henry wrote his best-selling refutation of Luther. His *Assertio Septem Sacramentorum* went through twenty editions, and was translated into most European languages. Two German editions reached Luther and stung him to respond.[2] Now Pope Leo X gave him the title and honour of *Fidei Defensor* - not just Defender of the Faith in England, but Defender of the Catholic Faith world-wide.

Watson grew up in a monastic world at Nun Stainton near Durham.[3] We know little about his earliest schooling, but for entrance to Cambridge he would have studied at Durham's Priory School. *The Rites of Durham*, written in about 1589 by an old man who perhaps knew Watson, recalls life in Durham Cathedral before the Dissolution. He describes the school, and the last schoolmaster, Robert Hartburne, as a venerable and learned monk, always looking for a bright pupil who was 'apte to lernyng, & dyd applie his booke, & had a prignant wyt wth all' to groom for university entrance.[4]

So, Watson grew up enjoying the magnificent setting, liturgy and traditions of Durham. When he left for St John's, Cambridge in 1529 he went from one Catholic powerhouse to another. The universities were academic extensions of the Church. The majority of staff and

Figure 1. Lincoln at the time of Bishop Watson. *Reproduced from J Williamson*, Guide Through Lincoln, *Lincoln, 1890.*

students, under their Chancellor the saintly John Fisher, were clerics or future clerics. University colleges were seedbeds for church leaders and tribunals or 'think tanks' for issues of the day. One such issue concerned Henry's decision to seek a 'divorcement' from Queen Catherine. The matter had gone to the pope, but he was prevaricating. Thomas Cranmer, a fellow of Jesus College Cambridge, suggested that Henry should consult the universities. If they found in his favour the pope would surely bow to their judgement![5]

So as Watson immersed himself in Greek and Latin Classics, the divorce issue raged around him. The first cracks began appearing in Anglo-papal relations. The serious breach came in December 1529 when Henry challenged papal authority in what came to be known as the *Reformation Parliament*. Cardinal Wolsey was stripped of his titles and offices, and with Fisher in disgrace for siding with Catherine, the university split into bitterly opposing factions; those for the king, and those for the queen and pope. During 1530 and 1531 the rift widened. When the pope ruled that Henry must neither divorce Catherine, nor marry Anne Boleyn, this was the last straw. The once obedient and dutiful son declared war on his Holy Father.

And so Watson, the young student, found himself drawn into a 'rebellion'. There were no doctrinal differences between the contenders. Henry was as Catholic as the pope himself. But when he began to question papal competence to interpret Leviticus, to issue a marital dispensation, or to pronounce unfavourably on his divorce, he was on a slippery slope. He was questioning, then denying papal authority itself.

Henry now judged those taking sides in terms of loyalty. No one could be allowed to recognise a higher authority than his. His *Act of Supremacy* was followed by the Submission of the Clergy in 1532. He could now appoint his own Archbishop to grant his divorce and ratify his marriage to Anne Boleyn. He found his man in Cranmer. By 1534 the last ties with Rome were broken. Now Henry looked to the loyalty of his subjects.

So it was that Watson was sucked into an escalating tragedy. Staff and students at Cambridge were required to take the Oaths of Supremacy and Succession. Fisher and others resisted and paid the penalty. There was no escape. In 1536 the twenty-one year old Watson further had to swear:

> *I will henceforth utterly renounce, refuse, relinquish, and forsake the Bishop of Rome, and shall accept, report and take the King's Majesty to be the only Supreme Head on earth of the Church of England.*[6]

What he thought of this he revealed in Latin verse, in a five-act play, based on Absalom's revolt against his father David in the Old Testament.[7]

His work, *Absalom*, was completed sometime around or soon after 1540 and was described in glowing terms by contemporaries for its literary and poetic brilliance. However, Watson wisely refused to publish it, and the manuscript was hidden and lost until rediscovered amongst sixteenth century humanist manuscripts in the British Museum in 1963.[8]

Absalom was written 'in trew imitation' of a classical tragedy, but with a contemporary twist. Nothing like it, in England, had been written before. In language and style it imitates Aristotle, Horace or Seneca, and yet in content the biblical story merges with events taking place all around.

The story begins with a prince quarrelling with his father. The issue concerns his brother and their relationship with a princess. Absalom demands a particular ruling from his father, but David cannot comply. Absalom decides to act in defiance of his father, and David censures him. Absalom flies into a rage, and furiously begins to undermine, then deny his father's authority.

Absalom's subjects are dismayed, but forced to take sides. Innocent people are sucked in. Absalom resorts to decrees, threats, intimidation and executions. Although he has qualms of conscience he overcomes them as opposition melts before his onslaught. With no father to restrain him, he can now do whatever he wishes.

The chorus in *Absalom* identifies David as God's elect, 'Son of Jesse', and anointed ruler of Israel. He unites diverse tribes into one people. He is their focus of unity with undisputed authority. He is holy and pious with a prayer always on his lips. He wants to help Absalom, but he cannot. He is full of love for his prodigal son. The chorus is not uncritical of David's weaknesses, but reveres his divine office as 'Holy Father' of God's people.

Similarly the chorus sees Absalom as David's once devoted son. He is a great prince with power and status derived from David. He had always honoured and obeyed his father according to the divine precepts. His very name 'Abba-shalom' means one who maintains peace with his father. But now he is acting like a spoilt child. If every whim is not granted he flies into a rage. Even his ministers go in fear, giving in to him in all things. But, warns the chorus, his unbridled pride symbolised by his 'fine physique' and 'long flowing hair caressing his broad shoulders', will be his downfall.

In *Absalom*, David presides over old Jerusalem as the pope presides over the New Jerusalem. The beloved son rebels against his father, launches his attack, overthrows him, and usurps his place. David refuses to retaliate, allowing time for Absalom to return to his senses and seek reconciliation. But Absalom sees his father's hesitation not as love, but as weakness.

In Watson's play, Absalom sacks David's temples in the territories he controls. He expels their guardians, loots their possessions, and destroys their altars.

There is no mention of temples in the Old Testament story, but what Watson describes matches the dissolution and the plundering of the monasteries, guilds, shrines and chantry chapels. Absalom is destroying David's last footholds, filling his treasury, funding his rebellion, and securing his own position. He vows there will be no reconciliation.

By Act IV those closest to Absalom are dismayed by his ferocity. He turns on these too, as Henry turned on Wolsey, Fisher, More and Cromwell. But opposition appears on two fronts. The disenchanted are converting back to David and joining those who had gone into hiding. And allies of David abroad are raising an army. No longer knowing whom he can trust, Absalom ruthlessly adopts a siege mentality. Those loyal to David are hunted down.

While the first four acts of *Absalom* look at parallels in what has happened so far, the fifth looks to parallels in the future. What happened to Absalom will happen to Henry. There will be a final battle. As victory went to David, it will inevitably go to the pope. As David resumed his appointed role over God's people, so will the pope. As Absalom's revolt amounted to nothing, nor will Henry's! A new monarch in England will prove more dutiful to the Holy Father than the turbulent Henry. Watson's message then, is one of patience, but total confidence in the ultimate victory of the pope.

And so Watson bides his time. He takes his Master's degree in 1537 and becomes a lecturer, then Dean of his college. However, with Cromwell as Chancellor after 1535, and Stephen Gardiner after 1540, the hunting down and purging of undercover papists is ongoing. Nicholas Metcalf, Master of St John's since 1518, is forced to resign in 1537. The next Master, George Day, is also denounced as a papist in 1538. Cromwell now has one of his own men, John Taylor, 'elected by force.'[9] He is the first avowed anti-papist 'reformer' to become Master of St John's College.

Taylor was Watson's worst nightmare. Encouraged by Cromwell, the rooting out of papists became a crusade. When he introduced a stiff vetting process for students and staff, Watson was one of twenty fellows to protest, but to no avail. When Cromwell was arraigned and executed for heresy in 1540, Taylor was also arrested. He was held for a while, but promised to conform to Henry's Six Articles. Heresy charges were dropped, and he resumed his office as Master.[10] But Lutheranism was on the increase. After Watson took his divinity degree in 1543, he began to emerge as one of the College's foremost champions and preachers of the Old Faith.

By 1545, with mounting hostility from Taylor and others, Watson consulted the Chancellor Stephen Gardiner. Gardiner, like Henry, was dismayed that anti-papal sentiment was becoming anti-Catholic as well. Whilst he had supported the king's efforts to overthrow papal authority in favour of royal supremacy he was now alarmed at where this might lead. Gardiner saw in Watson a kindred spirit and invited him to be his domestic chaplain – one of his personal aids. So in

1545 Watson joined the *familia* of the Bishop of Winchester and a new chapter opened in his life. He was no longer subject to Taylor, and now had the Chancellor's authority and support for his preaching. Within the year Taylor's zeal for reforming Cambridge was curbed. In 1546 he was forced to resign as Master of St John's.[11] Under Edward he would show his true Lutheran colours, and would follow Bishop Holbeach as the second (married) Protestant Bishop of Lincoln.

Watson worked side by side with Gardiner during Henry's last two years, trying to keep the Church in England Catholic. In the process he became widely known as a powerful advocate for the Old Faith. But it was a brutal age. During the last months of his reign, Henry ordered the execution of three papists for questioning his royal supremacy, and the burning of three Lutherans for questioning his Catholic doctrine.[12]

All was well while Henry lived and Gardiner held his own against Cranmer. But all was to change when Henry died.

Nine-year-old Edward VI came to the throne, and Protector Somerset became in effect the first Lutheran 'Head' of the English Church.[13] Some even called him a Calvinist.[14] When Gardiner opposed Somerset's changes he was arrested. Watson continued preaching but not for long. Two of Somerset's agents, Tonge and Ayre, who were appointed canons of Winchester in defiance of Gardiner, denounced Watson for hampering the cause of reform. Watson too was arrested and committed to the Fleet Prison.

In 1548 an amnesty was proclaimed and Gardiner and Watson were released.[15] But Gardiner was confined to house arrest in London and Watson stayed with him. In December they were allowed to return to Winchester. In their absence images had been removed from churches, the liturgy changed, processions forbidden, and Protestant preachers introduced. Henry VIII's Six Articles had been repealed, more changes were rumoured, and people were confused. Gardiner again protested. He and Watson were summoned back to London where Gardiner was recommitted to the Tower. But before he could be brought to trial the Lutheran Somerset had fallen, and the next effectual 'Head' of the Church was a Zwinglian; Protector Northumberland.

It was two years before Gardiner's trial. In 1551 Watson was called to give evidence for the prosecution and defence, and Gardiner was confirmed guilty. He was returned to the Tower where he stayed throughout Edward's reign. Watson was forbidden to preach, and may have paid a return visit to Durham. One story has him preaching in the north, being apprehended, and narrowly escaping the death penalty.

In December 1551 he was back in London to be examined on his belief in the doctrine of Transubstantiation. His examiners included no less than William Cecil, John Cheke, Robert Horne, and Edmund Grindal. His friends John Feckenham and John Young had also been summoned, and the examination took the form of a debate. The three were given assurances of immunity from prosecution, but were wary. Strype accuses Watson of equivocation. Grindal was furious with the outcome. At this time Watson was probably working with Gardiner on his case against Cranmer entitled *Confutatio Cavillationum*, printed in Paris in 1552.[16] This was later used against Cranmer at his trial. The fight went on.

When Mary came to the throne in August 1553 she immediately released Gardiner and restored him to his offices as Bishop of Winchester and Chancellor of Cambridge University. On Gardiner's advice she chose Watson to formally announce her intention to restore England to the Catholic Faith.

On 20 August 1553 a great gathering was called at St Paul's Cross. In the presence of the Queen, members of the court, bishops, dignitaries, nobility, the Lord Mayor and aldermen of London, representatives of the crafts and trades, and with a military guard, Thomas Watson stood to preach. It was more of a manifesto than a sermon. He referred to the confusion lately spread by Protestant preachers to whom people should no longer listen. He asked them not to seek new doctrines or a new faith, nor to build a new church or new temple. He exhorted them rather to return to the old faith, the Faith of their Fathers, and to help their Queen to restore the old temple. His sermon made a great impression, preparing the way for what was to come.[17]

Gardiner then sent Watson back to Cambridge with full authority to restore the University's former statutes and traditions. He was welcomed back, and elected Master of his old College, St John's on 28 September 1553. He confronted those Protestant members of Convocation who had expelled and excluded Catholics, and turned the tables on them. He reinstated the statutes of John Fisher, and committed the University to restoring and observing former Catholic traditions, customs and liturgies.[19]

But there were other pressing matters. Watson's beloved Durham Cathedral was in a state of chaos, and on 18 November he was elected its third Dean. Prior Hugh Whitehead, elected first Dean in 1540, had kept Durham Catholic under Henry VIII. At Edward's accession he was called to London and ordered to introduce the 'reformed' religion. He collapsed and died under the strain and was buried near the Tower of London.[20] Somerset then sent two 'commissioners' to Durham. The author of the *Rites* names them as Dr Harvy and Dr Whitby and describes their mission 'to deface all popish ornaments' not only in the Cathedral but in surrounding churches. A third villain was Dr Horne who delighted in trampling and desecrating Durham's shrines and ornaments under foot.[21] Robert Horne, Watson's old adversary, was appointed Dean in 1551. Now in 1553 Watson was sent to replace him. Horne hurriedly retired abroad.

It was a busy time for Watson. In April 1554 he went to Oxford to dispute or reason with Cranmer, Ridley and Latimer, now charged with heresy. He was also asked to examine other 'heretics', including Bishop Hooper and John Rogers, but was also in great demand for preaching. He was even summoned to preach before the Queen, which he did on 17 March and 14 April in *Two Notable Sermons*. The first was *Concerning the Real Presence of Christ's Body and Blood in the Blessed Sacrament* and the second *The Mass which is the Sacrifice of the New Testament*. These were really two lectures each taking several hours to deliver. He argued that the Early Fathers, the great Doctors, and the Councils of the Church witnessed to the truth of Catholic eucharistic teaching. He argued that the three bed-rocks of the Church had always been the scriptures, unbroken tradition, and the apostolic magisterium. Scripture alone was not enough – as sectarianism and fragmentation of religious belief after Luther had demonstrated.

Watson was passionate too about restoring the sacraments to those who had lost them. The more he preached the greater he was in demand. His engagements included several public orations like that at St Mary's Spital at the end of April. Mary was eager to relinquish her parliamentary title of 'Supreme Head on Earth of the Church of England', and seek reconciliation with Rome. Cardinal Pole, as Papal Legate, formally welcomed England back into the Catholic fold on St Andrew's Day, 30 November 1554. Watson had played a major part in this. His hopes and dreams so poetically expressed in *Absalom* had finally come about.

Bishop Gardiner, now convinced of the fatal flaw in royal supremacy, died reconciled to Rome in November 1555. John White, who had followed Taylor as Bishop of Lincoln, was translated to Winchester in 1556, and Thomas Watson, pending ratification by the pope, was elected the thirty-fourth Bishop of Lincoln.

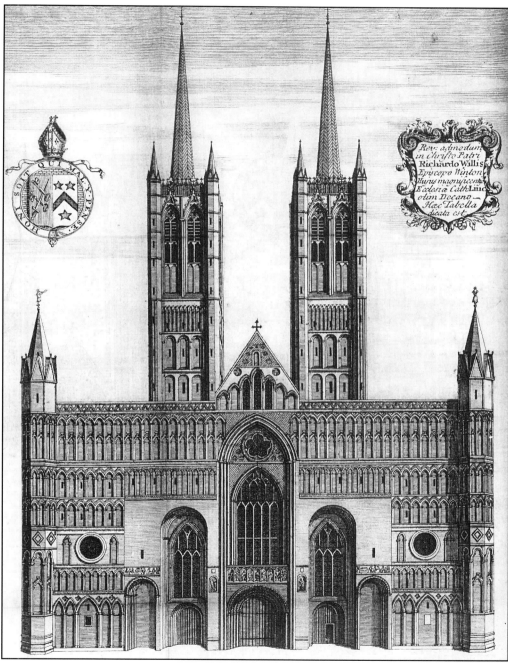

Figure 2. Lincoln Cathedral's Great West Doors. Thomas Watson was greeted by his clergy before these doors on the day of his consecration as Bishop of Lincoln on 15 August 1557. *Reproduced from B Willis, A Survey of the Cathedrals, Volume III, London, 1742.*

In January 1557, as Bishop Elect, he was sent by Cardinal Pole to 're-visit' Cambridge University and ensure that all was proceeding well. He was welcomed and invited to preach about the harm done by 'reformers' introducing unheard-of doctrines and ceremonies. He re-emphasised the importance of traditional doctrine, traditional symbolism and traditional liturgy.

The following month, February 1557, he officiated at the exhumation and burning of the remains of Martin Bucer and Paul Fagius. At the ceremony he preached for two hours on the harm they had done to the English Church by their 'wykedness and heretycall doctryn.'[23]

Watson's papal bull of appointment (the last ever for a Bishop of Lincoln) was issued on 24 March 1557. However, he still had business in Durham. On 29 May Cardinal Pole gave him permission to remain Dean of Durham for as long as necessary. His main task, the restoration of Catholic doctrine, customs and liturgy, included attempting to recover valuables, property and land plundered during the two previous reigns. But he also undertook some duties in the Diocese of Lincoln as Bishop-Elect.[24]

He was consecrated Bishop of Lincoln on the Feast of the Assumption of the Blessed Virgin Mary on the 15 August 1557 by

Figure 3. The arms of Bishop Thomas Watson incorporating those of the See of Lincoln. The serpents and doves in Watson's personal arms may be an allusion to Christ's words to his disciples, 'I am sending you out like sheep among wolves; so be as cunning as snakes and yet innocent as doves.' (Matthew 10:16). *Reproduced from T E Bridgett,* Sermons on he Sacraments, *Burns and Oates, 1876.*

the Archbishop of York in London.

Arriving in Lincoln for his installation in October, he was met with pomp and ceremony at the Cathedral's Great West Doors by his clergy. The bells rang out and the choirs sang angelically as he was conducted to his episcopal seat (Figure 2 and 3).[25] He was dismayed at the impoverishment of the diocese and set himself to recovering what he could, including several manors, estates and benefices seized by Henry and Edward. He also retrieved 'many rich vestments, articles of plate and other furniture of which the Church of Lincoln had been despoiled.'

Watson spent much of his time as Bishop of Lincoln travelling the diocese or in London (Figure 4). He was asked to preach at St Paul's Cross in February 1558 before another assembly of dignitaries, including the Lord Mayor and aldermen of London, ten bishops, and a huge crowd of people. In constant demand, he was now one of the hierarchy's most celebrated spokemen. At the request of Cardinal Pole and Convocation he prepared thirty of his sermons for publication. Entitled, *Holsome and Catholyke Doctryne concerninge the Seven Sacramentes of Chrystes Church, expedient to be known of all men, set forth in maner of Shorte Sermons to bee made to the People*, his book was printed in London in 1558.[27] Watson gained a reputation for leniency in dealing with Protestants. During his time as Bishop of Lincoln, the most severe period of Mary's campaign against 'heretics', there was not a single execution in the whole Diocese.[28]

Mary and Pole died, within hours of each other on the Feast of St Hugh of Lincoln, 17 November 1558. Elizabeth and Cecil lost no time in consulting with Protestant dissidents. In March 1559 the bishops were summoned to dispute with them over the future of the English Church. When it became obvious that the outcome was already determined, the bishops could not proceed. It was then alleged that White and Watson had urged them to consider the Queen's excommunication. The two bishops were arrested and sent by water via Traitors' Gate to the Tower on 3 April 1559.

By early May fresh *Acts of Supremacy and Uniformity* had been passed, and the Protestant *Book of Common Prayer* reintroduced. The bishops were once more cut off from Rome, stripped of their authority and 'extinguished' as a hierarchy.[29] On 25 June, Watson was tried, found guilty, deprived of his bishopric, and given a life sentence. One by one Elizabeth replaced the Catholic bishops with Protestants.

After a time in the Tower, Watson was placed in the custody of his old adversaries Grindal now Bishop of London, Guest, Bishop

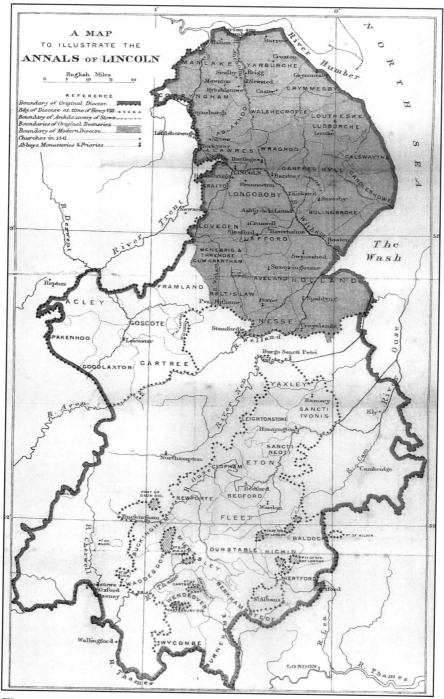

Figure 4. The changing boundaries of the Diocese of Lincoln. The original boundaries of the Diocese stretched from the Humber to the Thames. During the Reformation, just before Thomas Watson became Bishop, the Diocese's size was considerably reduced with the formation of the dioceses of Peterborough, (1541) and Oxford, (1542). Despite this, during Thomas Watson's brief time as Bishop of Lincoln, and for the following 300 years, the Diocese still comprises the counties of Lincoln, Leicester, Huntingdon, Bedford, Buckingham and part of Hertford.

Map reproduced from E Venables and G Perry, Lincoln: Diocesan History Series, *SPCK, 1897.*

of Rochester, and Cox, Bishop of Ely.

Ten years later, in 1570 the pope finally excommunicated Elizabeth. Watson was returned to the Tower. When interrogated about the excommunication his only regret was that it might create greater hardship for Catholics.[30] He was kept in the Tower until the following year, and then returned to former places of confinement. He was transferred from the Bishop of Rochester to the Bishop of Ely in 1580, and committed to the notorious Wisbech Castle Prison.

In one sense Wisbech Castle must have been a relief for the ageing Watson. The Bishop of Ely had turned it into something of a 'concentration camp' for Catholics, and for the first time in years he had friends around him. These included his old friend John Feckenham, fellow student at Cambridge, and the last Abbot of Westminster. Along with former Marian priests there were newly arrived seminary priests and Jesuits. His contacts now widened, and he appears to have exercised some sort of episcopal ministry *in vinculis*. He was in contact with the English Seminary at Douai, and it was reported that Jesuit militancy and inevitable repercussions worried him.[31] In March 1581 he was accused of corresponding with Catholics in Portugal, but his health and eyesight were deteriorating. He died almost blind at the age of sixty-nine. He had been confined for twenty-five years, ending his days in Wisbech Castle on 15 October 1584. He lies forgotten in an unmarked grave somewhere in the churchyard of Wisbech Parish Church. His only epitaph is given in the *Athenae Cantabrigiensis*.[32]

Thomas Watson, sometime Master of St John's College Cambridge,
Dean of Durham and Bishop of Lincoln:
Orator Facundas, Bonus Poeta,
Solidus Theologus et Concionator Celebris.
An eloquent speaker, a gifted poet,
a sound theologian and a celebrated preacher.

Notes and References

1. *Catholic Encyclopedia*, Volume VI, 'Golden Rose'.
2. J J Scarisbrook, *Henry VIII*, (Yale University Press 1997), p.113.
3. Thomas Baker, *History of the College of St John the Evangelist, Cambridge*, edited by John Mayor, (Cambridge University Press 1869), p.137.
4. 'The Rites of Durham', *The Surtees Society*, Vol 107, 1903, pp.96-97.
5. G de C Parmiter, *The King's Great Matter*, (Longmans, Green and Co Ltd. 1967), p.115.
6. T E Bridgett, *Sermons on the Sacraments by Thomas Watson*, (London Burns & Oates 1876), p.xxvi.
7. *2 Samuel*: Chapters 13 to 19.
8. John Hazel Smith, 'A Humanist's "Trew Imitation" ' : Thomas Watson's 'Absalom', *Illinois Studies in Language and Literature*, Number 52, 1964.

9. Baker, *History of the College of St John*, p.115.

10. Bridgett, *Sermons on the Sacraments*, p xxvii.

11. Baker, *History of the College of St John*, p.121.

12. Roland Bainton, *The Reformation of the Sixteenth Century*, (Hodder and Stoughton 1969), p.199.

13. Bainton, *The Reformation*, p 201.

14. A F Pollard, *Thomas Cranmer and the English Reformation 1489-1556*, (Frank Cass & Co Ltd 1965), p.185.

15. Bridgett, *Sermons on the Sacraments*, p xxxii.

16. Hazel Smith, 'A Humanist's "Trew Imitation" ', p.27.

17. G G Perry and J H Overton, *Biographical Notices of the Bishops of Lincoln*, (Lincoln Cathedral, George Gale, Lincoln 1900), pp.224-225.

18. C H Cooper and T Cooper, *Athenae Cantabrigiensis, Volume I, 1500-1585*, (Cambridge Deighton, Bell & Co 1858), p.492.

19. Baker, *History of the College of St John*, p.138.

20. 'The Rites of Durham', p.239.

21. 'The Rites of Durham', pp.69, 77 etc. Horne was blamed for widespread 'mischief and sacrilege' including the destruction of images and pictures of St Cuthbert – see chapters XXXIII, XXXV, and XXXVI.

22. Thomas Watson, *Two Notable Sermons Given the Third and Fifth Fridays in Lent Last Past Before the Queen's Highness*. Imprinted at London in Paul's Church Yard at the Sign of the Holy Ghost by John Cawood, Printer to the Queen's Highness: the tenth day of May 1554 (Copy in the Library of the Society of Antiquaries of London).

23. Cooper and Cooper, *Athenae Cantabrigiensis, Volume I*, p.492.

24. 'Chapter Acts AD 1547-1559', *Lincoln Record Society*, Vol.15, 1920, p.140.

25. 'Chapter Acts', p.144.

26. Perry and Overton, *Biographical Notices*, p.226.

27. The Library of Lincoln Cathedral contains a first-edition copy, but see also T E Bridgett, *Sermons on the Sacraments*.

28. 'Chapter Acts', p.xxvi.

29. G E Phillips, *The Extinction of the Ancient Hierarchy*, (London, Burns and Oates 1905).

30. Perry and Overton, *Biographical Notices*, p.227.

31. J J Scarisbrick, *The Reformation and the English People*, (Basil Blackwell 1984), p.139.

32. Cooper and Cooper, *Athenae Cantabrigiensis, Volume I*, p.494.

9. TECHNICAL EDUCATION FOR LINCOLN - 'A CITIZENS' UNIVERSITY'

by Jan Relf

*On behalf of the Committee to collect subscriptions for the
Building of a School of Science we beg to report in reference
to your resolution of January 1884 that we have now obtained
promises to the amount of £1966 0s 0d, which with the Government
Grant of £500 amounts to £2466 0s 0d... and inform us whether
your Committee are prepared to include Science in the Art
scheme. Will you bring this fact before your Committee...*[1]

THE ABOVE EXTRACT OF A LETTER from the School of Art
Building Committee paves the way for the formation of a new school
building for the School of Art which was founded in 1863, and
identifies the interest for a science faculty. The School of Art
Building Committee had authorised a Collecting Committee to
investigate whether a definite commitment from voluntary
subscribers existed for a new building for the School of Art. At the
same time a Science Committee was formed to investigate the
viability of opening a School of Science alongside Art, and what
potential there was to do so. The general trend towards the formation
of Schools of Science and Art was not only to improve technology,
but also to promote national prosperity.[2] A move for technical
education started in a piecemeal fashion with lone supporters such
as Lord Playfair in the 1860s who at one stage felt he was 'preaching
in the wilderness.'[3] The initiative to introduce technical education
was to continue to be 'weary and dreary work'[4], but staunch
advocates like Lord Playfair, Sir Philip Magnus, T H Huxley and
others meant that through voluntary efforts it was to play an
important part in the advancement of science and technology.

In 1884, when the Science Collecting Committee reported back to
the School of Art Building Committee, public subscriptions to the
value of £2466 had been raised and this mainly from two local
industrialists Nathaniel Clayton and Joseph Ruston.[5] The
government-created Science and Art Department in South
Kensington (1853) donated a further £350 demonstrating the
financial commitment offered to projects such as Lincoln's new

School of Science and Art.[6] The government was slow to become involved in organising and administrating technical education by keeping any legislation purely in the domain of elementary education. W B Stephens, notes that the government's preferred method of organising technical education was 'a more flexible one of indirect influence' rather than the 'continental model of direct control'. This left the development and organisation of technical provision to voluntary institutions 'providing part-time tuition for students already in work.'[7] The payment of a grant to an institution was not given randomly but was based on the recognition that the school was an 'organised science school' working towards national examinations.[8] Prize-giving, and course certification, were part of the educational structure of the School from the beginning. In 1923 Mr Collis, who had been an industrial draughtsman for Ruston, Proctor and Co., Lincoln before becoming headmaster of the Science faculty school in 1896, introduced National Certificates in Mechanical Engineering for apprentices employed by the city's engineering industries.[9]

The establishment of a Science School that was later to become a Technical College was due more to the commitment of industrialists and voluntary subscribers than to the state. It is important to recognise the tireless efforts made by certain local government councillors who were supportive of technical education, and were committed to the development of the School of Science and Art. The support given by local industries to the development of technical education in Lincoln was evident from the beginning, and during the formative years of its establishment industrialists remained significant contributors to its success. The commitment to develop technical education in Lincoln was finally secured with the granting of land by the Lord's Commissioners of Her Majesty's Treasury in June 1884 when they wrote allocating land 'containing 1790 sq. yds. from Monks Road to Cathedral Street' for the building of the School of Science and Art.[10] The eventual cost of the building £7,564 9s 8d had been raised by local subscriptions which included £600 donated by John Richardson, a director of Robey Ltd. The City Council donated £900 as a building grant for the new building on Monks Road which became the School of Science and Art and opened its doors to scholars from 27 September 1886 (Figure 1).

It is interesting to note that on the first evening a lecture was given by Dr Griffiths, the first headmaster of the science faculty, on 'Chemical Manures', a subject that he had been studying over the previous five years for the Chemical Society of London. The official

Figure 1. Gibney Building, Monks Road, Lincoln. *NLC Archives.*

inauguration of the School took place on 17 July 1887 and was performed by Lord Lieutenant of the County, The Rt Hon Earl Brownlow[11] in the grounds of the Sessions House where the mayor paid 'tribute to the trustees for their fund raising activities'.[12] A newspaper recorded the weather being 'brilliant' and the 'light and varied coloured dresses of the ladies having a charming effect.'[13]

The development of technical education was seen as fulfilling the educational needs of the working class sector and as the majority of students attending the School of Art came mostly from the 'the Artisan class'[14] an amalgamation between the two schools was seen as a sensible step. From its formation in 1886 the science faculty of the School of Science and Art enrolled 333 students in its first year studying 26 distinct science subjects. One student, A W Sissons, obtained a Whitworth scholarship worth £125 a year and tenable for 3 years.[15] The mayor F J Clarke, chairman of the committee for promoting the establishment of a School of Science, recommended in the first report that the building

> *should contain a Lecture Theatre which could be used in common by Students of both Schools, when occasion required. This Theatre should be made to accommodate an audience of not less than one hundred.*[16]

The report reflects the positive attitude taken by those individuals involved in organising the building of a School of Science and Art and the certainty that the school would attract a large student cohort from the local working-class community.

The establishment of a science faculty is seen to have developed from earlier initiatives to provide evening classes for artisans such as those provided by the Central School in 1873 and the Newland British School in 1875. The link in providing evening classes for adults goes further back to the establishment of the Lincoln branch of the Mechanics' Institute in 1833. W B Stephens acknowledges the fact that government policy in the nineteenth and early twentieth century left the provision of technical education to voluntary organisations like the Mechanics' Institute.[17] The Institute in Lincoln attempted to organise and provide evening classes for adult workers but was unsuccessful and by the 1870s its books and slates had been given to the Ragged School.[18] The abstract of accounts within the First Report acknowledged the reliance upon voluntary subscriptions and the awareness that not everyone supported the aims of the Institute.

> *too many consider the Institution, its Reading Room, its Books, its Lectures, its Conversation Meetings, as sources of mere amusement instead of stimulants to self-exertion; and thus neglect the advantage of what may be termed adult schools, in which by diligent application substantial progress is secured.*[19]

The attitude described may have resulted in the decline in donations and subscriptions, but Stephens views the decline in Mechanics' Institutes as being due to disorganisation whereas J W F Hill stated Lincoln's Mechanics' Institute 'outlived its usefulness'. The painstaking and valuable efforts of the Mechanics' Institute to improve the education and knowledge of the working class in Lincoln cannot be denied, but as technical and science studies became an increasing area of enquiry and debate a more concerted effort was necessary.

Formative years of technical education in Lincoln

The sitting of examinations and the attainment of certificates and prizes was to be a necessary incentive to studying courses at the school, and in the first syllabus of the Lincoln School of Science it stated

> *The Session will commence on September 27th, 1886, and will continue to May 1887, when the Students who have made their full attendance will be able to sit at the Government and Technological Examinations for Prizes, Certificates, Scholarships, and Medals, also the following of the City and Guilds London Institute:-*

| Honours | 1st Prize £5, and a SILVER MEDAL |
| | 2nd Prize £5, and a BRONZE MEDAL |

Pass	1st Prize £3 and a SILVER MEDAL
	2nd Prize £3 and a BRONZE MEDAL
	3rd Prize £2 and a BRONZE MEDAL
	4th Prize £1 and a BRONZE MEDAL[20]

Achievement was given a major focus, and presentation evenings were formally organised to acknowledge the success of students nominated for a prize. Absence was taken seriously and students were requested to 'attend regularly during the sessions, and to be in their places five minutes before the commencement of each Lecture.'[21] If the student did not meet the requirements set out by the governors of the School of Science the student would not be able to progress and sit their examination.[22]

Ralph Bates, a day time student in 1902 recalled his experience of studying science enthusiastically:

> *The physics laboratory under the direction of Mr Cooper was a wonderful place for me. Here we studied light and heat and, among other things, the design and construction of electric motors and dynamos.*[23]

Bates studied a variety of courses at the school 'he loved' that would equip him for later life, and in his letter, written in 1978, he recalls vividly the teachers and some of the implements that he made and still had in his possession.[24]

This letter demonstrates the impact that technical education made upon students and is borne out by the 1908 Board of Education report, which states 'no more serious type of student can be found

Figure 2. Class of 1903 Lincoln Technical School. *C V Middleton and Son, photographers.*

than the one who attends this school' (Figure 2).[25]

The presentation evenings were organised on a yearly basis with prizes and certificates presented by prestigious people such as Brigadier General Magnus Mowat who was the Secretary of the Institute of Mechanical Engineers and appeared in the 1936 brochure of the evening's event.[26] The choice of presenter was indicative of the status that was required to maintain the high calibre of technical education in Lincoln and its association with industry. By 1936 the prizes and certificates spanned a wider variety of subjects demonstrating the growth in student numbers and the development of science and traditional subjects within technical education, and although the prize money was less than in earlier years it remained a mark of individual student achievement. The college still maintained its reputation as a technical college but continued to expand by offering commercial courses such as book-keeping, shorthand and typing with academic studies in languages, English, history and geography.

In 1931 a newspaper, the *Lincolnshire Echo*, reviewing the past achievements of technical and art provision in Lincoln, stated that the college was 'among the most economically managed institutions of [its] kind in the country'. The success of the college was 'partly due to the excellent arrangements of the teaching staff, which are carefully and fully organised in the departments'.[27] The article proceeded to state that 'over 10,000 Lincoln people have been in attendance at the College during the last 25 years'. To a great extent this success was also due to the flexibility of training courses such as those designed for 400 female munitions workers in the engineering workshops during the 1914-19 period. The governors' enlightened attitude to training women can be seen in their 1918 report, which states that:

> *It is generally recognised that, in the future, women are going to take a larger part in the commercial and industrial life of the country, and no scheme can be regarded as satisfactory which does not provide for training in women's work.*[28]

Women had not only won the right to education by their war time actions but the freedom to vote by July 1918. John Stevenson remarks that in 1914 '212,000 women' were 'employed in engineering and munitions industries, but by 1918 the total was almost a million'[29] which demonstrates the scale of growth for women workers. The College governors were emphatic that evening and part-time day classes should be 'open equally to both sexes'[30] to reinforce the potential market that women reflected and the scope for future courses. The decision to offer courses for men and women demonstrated the visionary philosophy of gender equality held by the governors and those involved with planning courses, which was to be maintained and developed continually throughout the proceeding decades.

The report also acknowledged the improvements made to elementary and secondary education courses but stressed imperatives that 'Technical' and 'Commercial' classes should continue to meet 'the demands of the local industries' and that these courses should also

> *provide facilities for encouraging and securing intellectual development, by organising classes in Literature, Economics, Industrial History, and other humane studies which make for wise living and good citizenship.*[31]

It is recognised within this statement that education should not only prepare the working class for technical and commercial work, but that it should also enable the 'citizen' worker to live responsibly within the industrial, urban city. The college headmaster from 1896 to 1931, Mr Collis, also realised that 'citizenship' was inextricably linked to the development of industrialisation and urbanisation, and even in the post war economic restrictions pushed for funds to expand the buildings to accommodate a 'Citizens' University'. Progress and social mobility was central to Mr Collis' impassioned plea for continual expansion that would be advantageous to every 'ambitious son and daughter of the city', who possessed 'ability and grit to profit' from technical education.

The Technical College responded well to the war situation as Lincoln's industries went into full production manufacturing tanks and aircraft. Engineering firms introduced the pragmatic step of day release with pay for apprentices, which encouraged the growth of technical education with many firms paying school fees. The latter of these factors was a marked improvement on what existed previously when workers only had the option of training and education by attending evening classes sometimes still wearing their work clothes and tired from their day at work.

Local response to war was illustrated again in a Report by H M Inspectors in February 1947 which congratulated the College on its training courses to assist the war effort.

> *During the war the College did valuable work in the training of servicemen and civilians; 3,247 attended full-time and 10,024 part-time and evening. This adaptation to war needs tended to distort the organisation, which has been rather slow in re-adjusting itself.*[32]

The Report realistically emphasises the cost accrued by colleges such as Lincoln as it set aside routine courses to respond to the training requirements of a world war. Strategically Lincoln and its surrounding flat countryside played a crucial part in the war effort both in the use of land for airfields and in its industrial expertise in building engines for aircraft. The college, had also during the inter-war period trained and educated students, such as Mr H J Webb and Mr H P Baker, who were given posts as draughtsmen at the Royal Air Force Research Station at Farnborough in Hampshire. Both these men were only 23 years of age when they were selected from approximately 200 applicants, which is an accolade to their personal abilities and the education that prepared them for such a task.[33]

Even with its initial success the number of students attending courses at the School of Science and Art grew yearly together with the need for further buildings and workshops. In 1901 the school was proudly presented free of debt to the Corporation of Lincoln which owned the land, and was renamed 'The City of Lincoln Municipal Technical School'.[34] In 1928 the name was again changed to the 'Lincoln Technical College' and went under the management of a body of governors appointed by the Lincoln Education Authority with a full-time principal appointed. During this period the number of students attending engineering, science and commercial classes had increased from 333 in 1886 to 873 in 1926-7.[35] This rapid growth in student numbers reflects the industrial growth that had taken place in Lincoln throughout the later nineteenth century and early part of the twentieth century.

In 1932, with a new headmaster, Mr E R Walter, a former apprentice of Clayton and Shuttleworth and Chief Draughtsman at Nottingham National Projectile Factory, a new building was erected on Cathedral Street that contained workshops, laboratories, classrooms and lecture rooms. The College governors allocated the sum of £3000 so that the building would be well equipped for its purpose, but 'extremely generous gifts' continued to be given by local industries, ensuring further success for the college (Figures 3 and 4). The gifts given by industrial firms are clearly linked to industrial and technical courses:

1.	Ruston & Hornsby, Ltd	High speed diesel engine and loco boiler.
2.	Robey & Co., Ltd.	Two stage air compressor.
3.	W. Foster & Co, Ltd.	Centrifugal pumping set and tanks.
4.	Babcock and Wilcox, Ltd.	Two-stroke oil engine and boiler water wall.
5.	Ruston Bucyrus, Ltd.	Petrol paraffin electric lighting set.
6.	J & E Hall, Ltd., Dartford	Refrigerating plant complete.
7.	Armstrong-Siddeley Motors, Ltd.	Mounted aeroplane engine.
8.	National Gas Engine Co., Manchester	Gas engine.
9.	Crompton Parkinson, Ltd., Leeds	Switch gear and panel.
10.	Shipley & Co.	Wheelbarrow.
11.	James Dawson, Ltd., Lincoln	Belting.
12.	Duckerings Hardware, Ltd.	Piping and fittings.
13.	Richard Duckering, Ltd.	Brake gear.
14.	Ferranti Ltd., Hollingwood	Single phase house service electricity meter and a 2 1/2" two range moving coil voltmeter.[36]

The donations varied and were given by Lincoln firms and national companies. The minutes comment on the fact that the 'Donors have greatly helped with the erection of the plant and equipment, and in some cases they carried out the complete installation of their gifts'. This practical assistance given by industrial companies reinforces the viewpoints that further education and technical studies were still dependent upon voluntary subscribers.

Figure 3. Refurbished machine room in Cathedral Street Building 1932. *Lincolnshire Echo*

Figure 4. Cathedral Street Extension. *Lincolnshire Echo*

The role of further education 1945-1970

The *Education Act* of 1944 was in part a result of growing criticism from, amongst others, technical college principals and industrialists. They argued that the government had shown no concern for technical education as it had proposed minimal funding for the sector in the 1943 White Paper.[37] In the summer of 1945 the government-appointed Committee on Higher Technological Education produced a report which called for a radical policy to:

> *rapidly...expand the rising...status, prestige and level of 'a limited number' of local technical colleges which should develop courses comparable to university degree courses.* [38]

There was little attempt within the report to address the problem of technical education's low status, which it suffered despite its contribution to the economy since its emergence in the nineteenth century. As college courses had previously been designed for industrial and vocational needs it was now essential that students should be given the opportunity to specialise in courses that were comparable to degree courses. G D H and M I Cole commented in 1937 that

> *one of the most and least noticed facts of the modern world is the great increase in the number of persons who possess minor technical qualifications which are enough to raise them, both in their estimation and in their earning power, above the ruck of the unqualified or of those whose sole qualification is based on manual apprenticeship.* [39]

Technical education in Britain had played a crucial role in enabling people to train or study for jobs in industries and commercial sectors, but it remained a pragmatic solution based on self-help principles. The Committee for Higher Technological Education attempted to solve the divide between vocational and academic courses by improving the prestige of the former and bringing it in line with the elitist stature of the latter. The emphasis on changing attitudes to technical education came at a time when it was clear that Britain was still lagging behind other countries and had a much lower percentage of technicians and scientists in its workforce.[40]

The pessimistic view held by G W Roderick and M D Stephens that Britain's loss in world wide competition in technical and scientific innovation gained in the nineteenth century was due to 'no overall plan' by the government to education and research[41] is countered by W B Stephens when he argues:

Though direct state influence was minimized, financial aid was concentrated at the lower and intermediate levels on the part-time instruction of artisans and youths in technical and scientific principles [rather than on vocational training or more advanced work], *such provision being allowed to respond ad hoc to local industrial needs. Vocational training was left to employers and more advanced work and research to independent universities, industrial firms and others.*[42]

W B Stephens' argument recognises the duality of purpose evident within technical and scientific education. Lack of legislation for technical education had been evident in 1918 when Simon criticises the attitude of both industry and state bureaucracy for undervaluing 'technical education... at school and higher levels.'[43] Startling evidence remains of the period that out of three million school leavers aged 14 to 18 in 1918/19 only one in 25 attended part-time courses and one in 123 attended voluntary day continuation classes, which demonstrates that for many young adults further education or training was not possible.[44]

In January 1956, the prime minister Anthony Eden spoke in Bradford of the recognition that

prizes will not go to the countries with the largest population but those with the best systems of education will win. Science and technical skills give a dozen men the power to do as much as thousands did fifty years ago. Our scientists are doing brilliant work. But if we are to make full use of what we are learning, we shall need many more scientists, engineers and technicians. I am determined that this shortage shall be made good.[45]

Eden's speech acknowledged the merits of those people trained in the sciences and technology and that in them lay the future growth of the post-war country. The technological progress of the nineteenth century was built upon during the twentieth century with the development of weaponry, transport, aircraft, computers, communications, and space travel. From the 1950s onwards Britain and other major countries were destined to compete for scientific and technological prowess. The western world was becoming increasingly concerned with the outbreak of a nuclear war as relations between communist and capitalist countries deteriorated. It is in this post-war atmosphere that countries turned towards the development of science and technology in an effort to protect and maintain their dominance.

In response to Eden's call for further expansion in scientists and technicians, the college responded by further expansion in courses and buildings. A statistical report written by the principal, Dr Walters, showed an increase in students from 1,422 in 1938/39 to 2,000 in 1949/50, but by 1955 the numbers had increased to 2,524 students. Extensions and new buildings became an increasing preoccupation and during the next 30 years the college expanded rapidly to keep pace with the increasing student numbers. A newspaper reported in 1957 that students enrolling for courses had reached 3,500, so it is not surprising that in 1961 a new five storey building was added to the campus.

It was decided to open the Abbey Building in the Commonwealth Technical Training Week in 1961, and the ceremony reflected the optimism and pride associated with the College. The building cost £194,489 and was opened by the Lord Lieutenant of Lincolnshire, the Rt. Hon. the Earl of Ancaster.[46] The five storey building contained a library, kitchens, dining rooms, common rooms and class rooms for cookery, crafts and dressmaking on the first floor, commerce and academic studies on the second floor, and sciences

Figure 5. Abbey Street Building, 1961. *Lincolnshire Echo.*

Figure 6. Geography room, Abbey Building *Lincolnshire Echo.*

on the third floor (Figures 5 and 6). The ceremonial booklet produced for the event stated that the addition of Abbey Building to the College campus would equip it 'to take its part in the service of Further Education, a service of ever increasing importance to the country's economy and to the educational progress of its citizens.'[47]

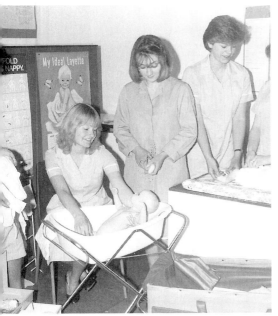

Figure 7. Nursing course. *NLC Archives.*

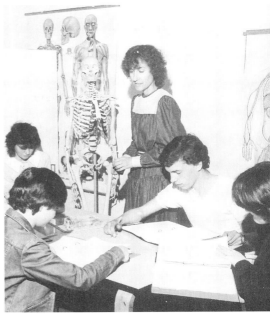

Figure 8. Biology room, Abbey Building. *NLC Archives.*

Figure 9. Electrical technicians, 1970s. *NLC Archives.*

Further Education in Lincoln from 1970 onwards

The expansion of the campus continued throughout the next three decades in an effort to meet the needs of a growing student group seeking a variety of courses, which included HNC Computing. This was offered for the first time in 1970. In an effort to respond to the needs of those people who were not able to attend a day or evening the College introduced 'Flexistudy' correspondence courses.[48] The 'Flexistudy' scheme had been introduced nationally and the College was keen to adopt this in an effort to accommodate the student living in either the city or the rural hinterland. The College continued to be dedicated to providing a flexible mode of delivery together with a breadth of courses. The College's commitment to both these factors can be demonstrated in the fact that if twelve or more people showed interest in a particular course then it would be included in the choice of subjects offered for that year.[49] In response to local requirements the College prospectus grew in range to include practical care courses such as Nursery Nursing, Nursing and Social Work from 1974 onwards (Figures 7 and 8).

The College's link with industry still continued throughout this period (Figure 9) and in 1984 training courses were designed for the workforce employed by the Lincoln-based Marconi Electronic Devices Ltd. Dr Crease, the new Dean of Technology and later Principal, spent a four month secondment investigating training programmes needed for the electronic industry.[50] The College continued with its commitment to training women when it introduced a programme entitled 'Women in High Technology'. This course was to discriminate positively on behalf of women in the field of technician engineer training.

The success of technical education nationally was not only down to the flexibility with which it responded decade by decade to industrial, economic, social, and political changes, but to local initiative, demand and support. (Figures 10 and 11) Technical education in Lincoln continued to prosper under the direction of many gifted and devoted teaching staff, but as Mr Collis remarked, without the response of ambitious local 'sons and daughters' the opportunity to proceed with education after secondary school would have faltered. Students throughout the history of the College have sought courses that would allow them to progress for personal and economic gain by technical, academic and commercial qualifications.

Between 1962 and 1993, three major initiatives challenged the College and one piece of legislation in particular was to have

Figure 10. Dressmaking room. *NLC Archives.*

Figure 11. Catering students in Abbey Building. *NLC Archives.*

profound implications on F E colleges nationally. A pragmatic step was taken in 1962 to establish two separate boards of governors instead of the one board that had operated since the introduction of the science faculty in the Art School. Although both colleges had been independent of one another for a considerable time, the decision to split the governors into two boards was a result of the success and growth of both the Lincoln School of Art and Lincoln Technical College. Arthur Ridings, College Principal, in his 1986 centenary letter spoke of extending the college 'service to the wider community throughout Lincolnshire while at the same time maintaining its contact with the working city as a base of its operation'.[51]

In the light of this message a merger took place with Gainsborough College of Further Education and the Louth centre in an effort to provide an effective and viable further educational service in Lincolnshire. Consequently, the institution changed its name to North Lincolnshire College. With its increase in size, the College ensured its position as the largest provider for post-16 technical and academic education in the area.

The impact of the *Further and Higher Education Act* of 1992 was to create major implications for all further education colleges as they moved from local authority control to become independent organisations with charitable status.

From 1993 North Lincolnshire College was to continue this transition by moving from a board of governors made up of local authority members to one which was predominantly business orientated. Although the College continued to offer a wide variety of competitive courses, and to attract growing numbers of new students the management was severely challenged by their new status. Colleges, such as North Lincolnshire College, were to continue their struggle for recognition and equality in a highly competitive educational market where compulsory schools and higher education institutions gained increased funding and enjoyed a more prestigious political platform.

Since 1993 further education colleges have struggled financially, endured cut backs, and redundancy, but colleges such as North Lincolnshire College have managed to operate efficiently by maintaining their flexibility and high standard of delivery in all subject areas, while keeping abreast of current changes and initiatives.

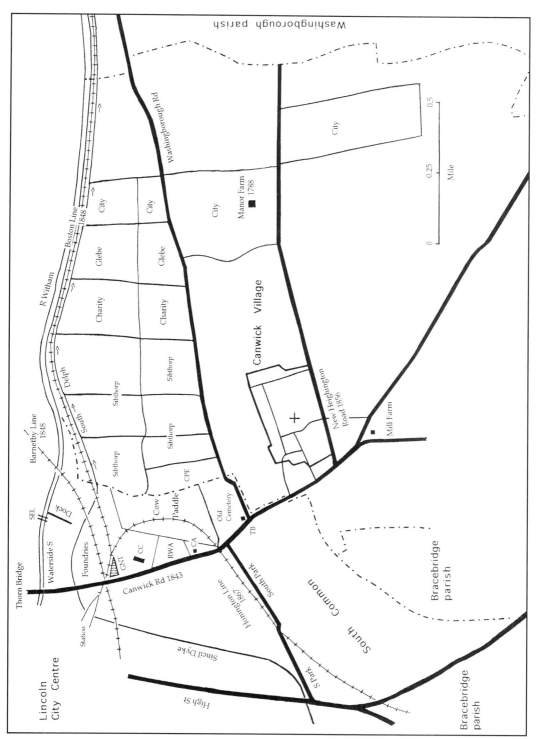

Figure 4. Map of the area based mainly on Figure 3 and the J S Padley's Lincoln city plans of 1851 and 1868. Abbreviations (1) CA - *Chaplin Arms*; CC - Clarke's Crank Works; CPE - Cow Paddle extension; GNT - Great Northern Terrace; RWA - Robey's Works area; SEL - Stamp End Lock; TB - Toll Bar cottage, 1843. (2) Landowners are given as follows: Sibthorp (of Canwick Hall); City (Lincoln City Council); Charity (Garratt's Charity); Glebe (Canwick Glebe Farm - Mercers' Company and the Vicar). *Map drawn by Joan Mills.*

The Canwick enclosure award of 1787 defined a boundary, placing the common in the city and the other areas in Canwick. The Canwick-Lincoln boundary so established remained in position down to 1967, despite the fact that many urban uses had long since taken over large sections of the lower part of Canwick parish. In that year the boundary was moved to run along the south side of Washingborough Road, but diverging further south to take in the whole of the Sewage Farm, then running north to join the river along the farm's eastern limit (Figure 6).[5]

Roads between Canwick and Lincoln

There was freedom of movement on foot between Lincoln and Canwick across the common and on footpaths crossing the Bargate Closes which, for most of their length, separated the common from the Sincil Dyke. For wheeled vehicles the route was less direct, requiring a journey all the way down the High Street to the Great Bargate. It then crossed Canwick Common on a line similar to that later taken by the road named South Park. At the east end there was a southward turn to start the ascent of Canwick Hill, just short of the line of the present Canwick Road. Another turn, this time eastwards, just north of the site of the Toll Bar cottage (1843), took the traveller to Washingborough. That course is now followed by a drive through the Old Cemetery. When the cemetery was laid out, Washingborough Road was moved southwards to its present position on the south side of the Toll Bar cottage (cf. Figures 3 and 4).

In 1777 the turnpikes on the south side of Lincoln were extended, including the stretch of road from Bargate across the common. Under the 1784 Act the turnpike was also extended up Canwick Hill, as far as the mill (a point now marked by Mill Lodge). But a direct route to Canwick was still in the future and our study area was still served only by Waterside South and Washingborough Road.[6]

All this was to change in the early 1840s, because the High Bridge was getting jammed by horse-drawn traffic. There were narrower bridges at the Brayford Head and at Thorn Bridge (a swing bridge), but no road struck out across the closes, mainly because these were subject to flooding. In 1839 a scheme first discussed in 1833 was revived, whereby Canwick Road, including Melville Street and Pelham Street, was built on a ramper and a 'new toll bar was placed at the junction of the Branston and Washingborough Roads, on Canwick Common'. Canwick Hill was lowered, above the point where the city boundary crosses the road. It is also possible that an improvement had occurred in 1777.[7]

Figure 5. Postcard based on a drawing of 1854. The viewpoint was on South Common, to the west of that used for Figure 1. The Royal Agricultural Society held its 1854 Meeting in Lincoln and the showground was located on the Cow Paddle. Note the toll bar and cottage at the bottom of Canwick Hill and the lack of development on either side of Canwick Road, on the left hand side of which the hospitality tents of the Show can be seen in the Bargate Closes. The horizontal lines in the middle distance represent the river Witham and the Boston railway line. The postcard was issued c1900 by W J Smith of 44 Canwick Road, based on an engraving published on page 60 of the *Illustrated London News*, 22 July 1854. *Card by courtesy of Maurice Hodson.*

Developments on the eastern margin of Canwick Road

Although Canwick Road and South Park became a relief route for the High Street, there was not much development along Canwick Road south of the railway crossing for a long time after the road was built. Developers were, no doubt, deterred by the danger of flooding. On the east side of the road only the *Chaplin Arms* was marked on Padley's 1851 map. The area was so empty of development in 1854 that it could be used for the Royal Show of that year (Figure 5). The first part of Clarke's crank works was erected in 1859. A few houses had appeared by the time of Padley's 1868 revision, and this shows the major development of the first section of Robey's works, probably in 1864. Comparison with Padley and Thropp's map of 1883 indicates that the works area had been extended up to the edge of the Honington railway line by the later date. Also most of the

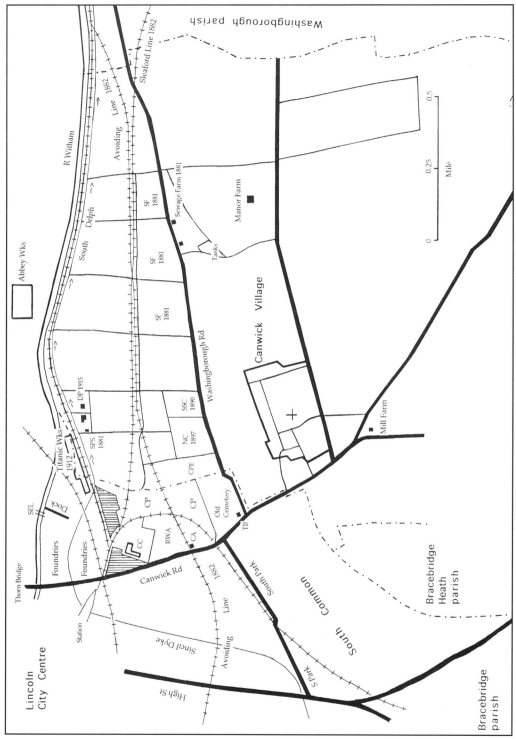

Figure 6. Map of the area c1914, based mainly on Padley maps, with information later than 1883 from OS maps. Abbreviations as follows: CA - *Chaplin Arms*; CC - Clarke's Crank Works; CP - Cow Paddle; CPE - Cow Paddle extension; DP - Destructor Plant; NC - New Cemetery; RWA - Robey's Works area; SEL - Stamp End Lock; SF - Sewage Farm; SPS - Sewage Pumping Station; SSC - St Swithin's Cemetery; TB - Toll Bar cottage, converted to a cemetery lodge; vertical shading - residential streets. *Map drawn by Joan Mills.*

terraced streets east of Canwick road (cleared since c. 1960), including those lying off Great Northern Terrace, were built in the period 1868-83 (Figure 6).[8]

Railways

The Boston-Lincoln line was constructed on the south bank of the Witham in 1848, but entered the city on land between the South Delph and the site of the Titanic Works. In the same year the line from Barnetby was built across the northern edge of the area. The Lincoln-Honington railway line opened in 1867. Emerging from the south through Bracebridge, it ran eastwards partly across the Bargate Closes, but mainly on the northern fringe of the common. Then it swept across the Cow Paddle in a curve still visible, for instance in the eastern boundary of Tesco's car park (Figures 4 and 6).

The construction of the Lincoln-Sleaford line and the high-level avoiding line across the middle of the area occurred in 1882. The bed of a short connection between the Boston line and the high-level line survives with a large bridge over the South Delph. Thus stretches of five different railway lines carved up the area, disastrously from an agricultural point of view, and made movement difficult for other purposes. Apart from flood dangers, the building of foundries and related working-class housing was still inhibited by the absence of good road access.[9]

Cemeteries

In 1847 a gravedigger, digging a grave in St Benedict's churchyard, threw out a ten-year old coffin, the yard being full to overflowing. The coffin fell apart revealing bones accidentally observed by the dead man's widow.[10] This incident brought to a head the public health problem of churchyards, as most were in the same state (and many others in expanding cities all over the country). St Swithin's parish had already acquired a new site in Rosemary Lane. Under the *Public Health Act* of 1848 further moves were started, but procrastination led to the intervention of the government's Board of Health, whereby all Lincoln churchyards below hill were to be closed by October 1854.

The Old Cemetery was opened only in 1856. The sixteen acres of land cost £1,150 and the whole expense amounted to nearly £6,000 for land, landscaping, construction of the chapel and lodge, and equipment. Hill describes the inter-denominational struggle over the mortuary chapels and the distribution of consecrated (Anglican) ground in relation to flood levels. Only one chapel was erected. It was Anglican at the west end with a tower and a bell, and nonconformist at the east end. There is also a Roman Catholic area within the cemetery, near the east gate.[11]

The Old Cemetery was established on common land and Robey's acquired a further 6.75 acres of the Cow Paddle. Only in 1868 did the city council obtain a private Act to legalise these changes retrospectively. The commoners were compensated with 17.5 acres of land in Canwick, adjacent to the east side of the Old Cemetery. This area is still common land (Figures 4 and 6).[12]

Kelly gives 1890 as the date for the opening of St Swithin's Cemetery and 1897 for the New Cemetery. These dates are confirmed by the timing of land sales by the Sibthorp estate to the burial boards, in 1890 for St Swithin's and 1896 for the New Cemetery, the latter costing £250 for nearly eleven acres. All the cemeteries were taken over by the city council in 1907.[13]

Sewage Farms

In 1849 the first report was published in which a need for underground sewerage was expressed. The death rate was 24 per 1000 persons per annum, above the threshold of 23 per 1000 needed if the 1848 *Public Health Act* were to be invoked. During the 1860s the death rate in Lincoln was rising, and very high for a town of its size. In 1873 the council bought land for (sewage) irrigation near Great Northern Terrace, and in anticipation of the next move. However, progress was so slow that the High Court intervened to make the council move expeditiously and in 1876 the contract was signed for the underground sewerage to be constructed.

In 1881 pumping began, with all sewage converging on the Great Northern Terrace site, which was used in association with the Washingborough Road site from the very first. The latter already belonged to the city council as part of their Manor Farm, but the Great Northern Terrace site had to be purchased from the Sibthorps' Canwick estate (Figure 6).[14]

In 1920 three Lancashire steam boilers were being used to drive the pumps which ran normally at 14 strokes a minute, each stroke pumping about 145 gallons. The bottom of the sewage well was 23 ft below the ground and the sewage was lifted 60 ft above the floor of the station (presumably to the tanks on Washingborough Road). In dry weather the throughput would be about 2.2 million gallons per day, rising to as much as six millions after heavy rain.[15]

On the site today are a pair of cottages and the two principal buildings of 1881. The latter were not sold to Joseph Nugent Ltd until 1985 when pumping from Washingborough Road replaced pumping to that site from this one. The nearer building is used as Nugents' offices. In front, across the road, a very large manhole cover marks the point where the main sewer now starts its course to the Washingborough site, having been diverted away from Nugents in 1985. The second building is their workshop where they produce electrical and pumping equipment. Coincidentally, this was the pump house containing steam engines (replaced by diesels before 1985), with the root of their chimney stack still visible.[16]

Next to these buildings was the destructor plant, which Nugents demolished, and beyond this can still be seen the original tanks. These passed on liquid to the filter beds to the right (south), in the area now used as the Household Waste Disposal Site. The destructor plant was probably set up as a result of Alderman Pratt's lecture to the city council in 1904 on the subject of fly-tipping on the commons and on waste disposal. Hill states that provision was made for the destructor plant in 1911, but it was not opened until 1915. It was capable of dealing with all the City's waste, and the steam so generated was used for driving the sewage pumps next door.[17]

Old Ordnance Survey maps offer some clues as to other

Figure 7. A postcard of the Sewage Farm used postally in 1905. Irrigation is the centre-piece, with fruit trees to either side, and the line of Washingborough Road picked out by the farm buildings and cottages; beyond is the Heighington Road area of Canwick parish. *Postcard by W J Smith, courtesy of Maurice Hodson.*

developments. The 1887 six-inch map shows at Washingborough Road one set of sewage tanks on the hillside, with fruit trees below on both sides of the road (Figure 7). In 1905 the area covered by tanks was much larger. The land between the Canwick boundary and the pumping station in Great Northern Terrace was used as allotments, as in 1932. At both dates the five fields or so east of the Terrace filter beds were used for irrigation purposes. Today the first field contains a scrap-yard belonging to the city council, but the first two or three fields are mostly covered with grassed-down spoil heaps about fifteen feet high. The more easterly pair are also grass fields, some of the area still covered by rough grass indicative of the sludge beds. In the 1960s there was considerable expansion of the tanks and filter beds at Washingborough Road, but irrigation appears to have come to an end about that time.

The Titanic Works
As the industrial development of Lincoln progressed, good industrial sites near river, canal, and/or railway became scarce close to the city centre. Consequently, new foundries were built at Boultham, and also further downstream on the banks of the Witham. The Titanic Works were built partly in Lincoln, partly in Canwick parish (Figures 1, 2 and 6). It is generally accepted in Lincoln that these works were so named because they were constructed at the same time and to the same length as the liner Titanic.[18] However, the building's length is considerably greater than the liner's, which was 883 ft. Measurement from the OS 25-Inch plan of 1932 shows the extreme length of the works then was 1,167 ft; excluding what may have been later additions yields a figure of 1,000 ft, which tallies with two published measurements.[19]

Clark gives 1912 as the date of erection and states that the Titanic Works were at first used jointly for steam (road) wagon production and railway rolling stock. When Clayton Wagons Ltd was formed soon after the first world war, rolling stock production was transferred across the river to the Abbey Works, and the Titanic Works concentrated on steam wagons, of which Claytons made 1,200 between 1912 and 1929. The choice of name seems faintly ludicrous: even if it had been chosen before the liner sank, surely such a bad omen ought to have forced a change of mind.[20]

Conclusion
The expansion of urban – or at least non-agricultural uses of land - has gradually taken up virtually the whole of the study area. Land

uses requiring good roads were discouraged by inadequate road access, a factor compounded by obstacles presented by the rail network. Another powerful factor was proximity to a river that could not be entirely trusted. When surface drainage came to be a less vital issue, the use of a large area for sewage disposal was enough to deter residential development.

Today, poor road access is still a significant issue, made more intense by the recent establishment of the Lincolnshire Road Car bus depot near the Titanic Works. This traffic has to cross the railway in Great Northern Terrace, where severe delays are currently threatened by the proposal to route many more freight trains through Lincoln. Lack of bridges over the South Delph and the river Witham are also a notable impediment to movement across the area. A new road to link Monks Road with the junction of Canwick Road and South Park Drive, running to the east of the Tesco store and the Household Waste Site would be a considerable improvement.

Although the Sibthorps were able to sell land for urban purposes in the lower part of Canwick parish, these uses were to limit the exploitation of their other land in the valley for residential purposes. In this sense, the experience of the Canwick estate sharply contrasts with that of the Ellison estate at Boultham, which was overrun by suburban expansion after 1918. By comparison, although Canwick is a commuter village, it is still insulated from Lincoln's built-up area.

Acknowledgements and abbreviations

I wish to acknowledge the assistance given to me by the staffs of Lincoln City Council, the Lincolnshire Archives Office (LA), Lincoln Central Library (LCL), and the Usher Gallery (UG). Help and encouragement has also come from Neville Birch, Maurice Hodson, Ray Hooley, Neil Wright, and my wife, Joan Mills. My particular thanks to Poppy Griffin and Andrew Wyld of Agnew's Gallery are recorded in connection with Figure 2.

Notes and References

1. Sir Francis Hill (1974), *Victorian Lincoln*, especially pp. 118-25 and pp. 201-02; N R Wright (1982), *Lincolnshire Towns and Industry 1700-1914*, chapter 6: and D R Mills, ed. (1989), *Twentieth Century Lincolnshire*, chapter 4, especially the map of factories, Figure 4.2.
2. W H Wheeler (1868), *A History of the Fens of South Lincolnshire* (enlarged 1896 edition reprinted, 1990), pp. 152, ff; Sir Francis Hill (1966), *Georgian Lincoln*, pp. 131-36; Hill, *Victorian*, pp.96, 205, 214; Wright, *Towns and Industry*, p.226; J S Padley (1882), *Fens and Floods of Mid-Lincolnshire*, pp.53-9.
3. Samuel Buck - *Lincoln from Mr Dickinson's summer house at Canwick*, UG 465.
4. Sir Francis Hill (1948), *Medieval Lincoln*, p. 355; manorial records - Lincolnshire Archives (LA), LC Charters Box 20/419.
5. Enclosure award - LA, Canwick Par 17; information on 1967 changes from Lincoln City Council, courtesy of C Keywood.

6. Wright, *Towns and Industry*, p.259, Hill, *Georgian*, p.123; LA, LLHS 43/2/1.

7. Hill, *Victorian*, p.62.

8. Hill, *Victorian*, p.120; Lincoln Central Library (LCL) filing references for Padley's maps are: 1819 - 509, 509a; 1851 - 865; 1868 - 870, 886; 1883 - 887; for the 1842 map see LA, EX 30/6. Clarke's Crank Company survives on the same site to-day.

9. J G Ruddock and R E Pearson (1974), *The Railway History of Lincoln*; Wright, *Towns and Industry*, appendix III, and Hill, *Victorian*, p.209.

10. Hill, *Victorian*, p.159.

11. Hill, *Victorian*, p.159-60; W. White, ed. (1872), *History, Gazetteer and Directory of Lincolnshire*, pp.20 and 35 of 1988 reprint.

12. Hill, *Medieval*, p.357.

13. Kelly and Co. (1922), *Directory of Lincolnshire*; land sales - LA, BS3 Canwick/3/3 and 4; Hill, Victorian, p.360. East of St. Swithin's Cemetery, the crematorium was opened in 1968 - B M Short, ed. (1990), *A Bibliography of Printed Items relating to the City of Lincoln*, Lincoln Record Society, Vol. 79, item 2547. The land to the east of the crematorium also belongs to the city council. It is leased to the Lincoln Ten-Pin Bowling Centre which established a golf driving range in 1980 and the first part of the bowling centre 10 June 1983 - information from the manager, April 1997.

14. Hill, *Victorian*, pp.161-170.

15. Institution of Mechanical Engineers (IME) (1920), Lincoln Meeting 1920: Notice of Works Open to Members, p.10 (LCL, at L.621, brochures, etc in envelope).

16. Information from Joseph Nugent Ltd, March 1997.

17. E Pratt (1904), 'City of Lincoln. Town's refuse, its destruction and uses', (paper read to Lincoln Corporation, 22 April 1904, copy in LCL at L.Linc. 614); Hill, *Victorian*, p.240; IME, Lincoln Meeting, p.9.

18. e.g., A Muir (1958), *Seventy-Five Years. A Record of Progress: Smith's Stamping Works (Coventry)*, Smith-Clayton Forge, Lincoln, p.61; J Walls (1977), *Clayton and Shuttleworth and Marshall Aircraft Production*, p.3.

19. M H Watson (1987), *Disasters at Sea*, p.499; R H Clark (1963), *The Development of the English Steam Wagon*, p.90; and IME, Lincoln Meeting, p.15.

20. Clark, *Steam Wagon*, p.90; R Brooks and M Longden (1986), *Lincolnshire Built Engines*, p.9.

11. PLEASURE EXCURSIONS FROM LINCOLN 1846-1914

by Eleanor Nannestad

FROM THE MID-NINETEENTH CENTURY onwards, taking a day's pleasure excursion became a popular leisure activity, particularly among the working classes. It was a novelty, as trips of this kind had not been possible in the early nineteenth century, and it was the fashionable thing to do. As local newspapers testify, Lincoln people were caught up in this trend, for not only did they travel on excursions themselves, but also the city was a popular destination for trippers from elsewhere. This chapter seeks to examine the factors contributing to the growth and development of the excursion phenomenon from the mid nineteenth century to the outbreak of the First World War, with examples taken from Lincoln newspapers.

By the 1840s the effects of industrialisation had reached Lincoln, almost a century later than many other midland and northern cities. Until the 1840s, Lincoln had been an agricultural market town, but with the opening of four large foundries (Clayton and Shuttleworth in 1842; Robey in 1854; William Foster in 1856; Ruston, Burton and Proctor in 1857)[1], plus several smaller industrial enterprises, the city's economy became dependent on the manufacturing industry and its population trebled between 1831 and 1881.[2] By 1871, nearly ten per cent of the city's total population were employed in iron manufacture.[3] It was these people and their families who benefited from the social changes which enabled the working classes to enjoy excursions.

In order to take a day trip, people would need the time to go, the money to be able to afford their fare, and the transport to take them to their destination. All these things became available to the working family in the course of the nineteenth century.

Firstly, the time: during the nineteenth century, traditional patterns of working hours changed for many working-class people, mainly because of industrialisation. Unlike the agricultural worker, whose hours were dependent on the seasons and the hours of daylight available, those employed in factories could work long shifts in both summer and winter, as factories could be kept in operation round the clock to maximise profits. The exploitation of workers in this way by unscrupulous factory owners led to a series of *Acts of Parliament* being passed throughout the century. These sought to regulate the number of hours worked, firstly by women and children and later by men. As the nineteenth century advanced, working hours were reduced.[4] By the late 1850s, factory workers commonly had a half day holiday on Saturdays, finishing work at lunch time. This gave them an afternoon which could be spent on leisure or recreation.[5] By the late 1880s Lincoln shops closed early on a Wednesday, allowing their employees a half day off, thus affording the possibility of a trip to a local sports fixture or a bicycle ride round a nearby village. A trip to the coast was also possible as by that time afternoon trains were running from Lincoln to Skegness, catering for those who wanted a half day trip.[6] Most people regarded Sunday as a day for rest and church (even if they didn't attend themselves), so excursions were not generally run on that day, although Sunday trains were operating by the late nineteenth century.

In 1871 the *Bank Holiday Act* was passed designating the first Monday in August as a national holiday. As this new holiday fell at the warmest time of year, when daylight hours were long, and it was not a religious festival with the attendant obligation to go to church, it provided an ideal opportunity to take a day's excursion. In addition, in many areas it became a tradition to take local holidays, such as the Lancashire Wakes. In Lincoln, the last Saturday in July, known as 'Trips Saturday' became one of the most popular days for an excursion.

By the mid-nineteenth century, many people had not only enough to buy the essentials of life, but a little left over which could be spent on leisure activities. Factory workers were always paid more than agricultural workers, and throughout the century wages generally were rising. It has been estimated that between 1850 and 1900, they rose by about 75 per cent in real terms.[7]

However, it was the arrival of a new form of transport, the railway, which brought the possibility of cheap, fast travel over a long distance to large numbers of people. Lincoln's first railway line opened on 3 August 1846, running from the old Midland, later St Mark's, station (closed in 1985 and subsequently demolished) to Newark, Nottingham and Derby. Within a week of opening , trains were taking people to the Nottingham races, offering a return journey for the price of a one-way fare.[8] Outings by horse drawn vehicles had always been possible, but there was a limit to the distance that could be travelled this way in a day. Steam vessels, which appeared in the early nineteenth century, could convey large numbers of people over long distances within a day, so that for those who lived near a sea or river port, possibilities of travel to new destinations were opening up. From around 1814, a steam packet, travelling at around eight miles an hour, ran along the river Witham between Lincoln and Boston, carrying passengers travelling for pleasure as well as business.[9] The train, however, travelled faster and carried more passengers than the steam vessel, and became the popular mode of travel for working people and as result it was places accessible from the rail network that became the most popular destinations for the Victorian excursionists.

Thus as the century progressed, many of Lincoln's working people had increasing leisure time, a little money to spare and a convenient rail service to many destinations. They were better placed both geographically and economically to take excursions than their rural counterparts.

As the rail network spread, more destinations opened up to Lincoln excursionists. Cheap trips to London were reported in 1847, and after the opening of the Great Northern (later the Central) Railway Station in St Mary's Street in 1848, it was possible to travel to Grimsby.[10] A popular outing was to take the train to Grimsby, then either to walk the two miles to Cleethorpes or to take a horse drawn omnibus. It was not until 1863 that the railway was extended from Grimsby to Cleethorpes, making Cleethorpes the first Lincolnshire seaside resort accessible by rail.[11] Throughout the Victorian period, Cleethorpes was always the most popular resort with Lincoln people, although Skegness became a close second after a railway line was opened there in 1873 (Figure 1). Mablethorpe could be reached by rail in 1877 and Sutton on Sea in 1886.[12] All

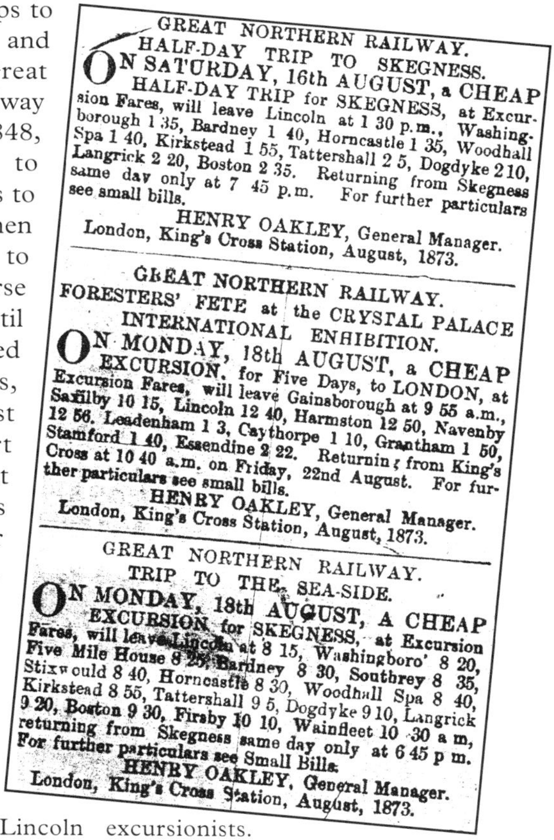

GREAT NORTHERN RAILWAY.
HALF-DAY TRIP TO SKEGNESS.
ON SATURDAY, 16th AUGUST, a CHEAP HALF-DAY TRIP for SKEGNESS, at Excursion Fares, will leave Lincoln at 1 30 p.m., Washingborough 1 35, Bardney 1 40, Horncastle 1 35, Woodhall Spa 1 40, Kirkstead 1 55, Tattershall 2 5, Dogdyke 2 10, Langrick 2 20, Boston 2 35. Returning from Skegness same day only at 7 45 p.m. For further particulars see small bills.
HENRY OAKLEY, General Manager.
London, King's Cross Station, August, 1873.

GREAT NORTHERN RAILWAY.
FORESTERS' FETE at the CRYSTAL PALACE INTERNATIONAL EXHIBITION.
ON MONDAY, 18th AUGUST, a CHEAP EXCURSION. for Five Days, to LONDON, at Excursion Fares, will leave Gainsborough at 9 55 a.m., Saxilby 10 15, Lincoln 12 40, Harmston 12 50, Navenby 12 56, Leadenham 1 3, Caythorpe 1 10, Grantham 1 50, Stamford 1 40, Essendine 2 22. Returning from King's Cross at 10 40 a.m. on Friday, 22nd August. For further particulars see small bills.
HENRY OAKLEY, General Manager.
London, King's Cross Station, August, 1873.

GREAT NORTHERN RAILWAY.
TRIP TO THE SEA-SIDE.
ON MONDAY, 18th AUGUST, A CHEAP EXCURSION for SKEGNESS, at Excursion Fares, will leave Lincoln at 8 15, Washingboro' 8 20, Five Mile House 8 25, Bardney 8 30, Southrey 8 35, Stixwould 8 40, Horncastle 8 30, Woodhall Spa 8 40, Kirkstead 8 55, Tattershall 9 5, Dogdyke 9 10, Langrick 9 20, Boston 9 30, Firsby 10 10, Wainfleet 10 30 a m, returning from Skegness same day only at 6 45 p m. For further particulars see Small Bills.
HENRY OAKLEY, General Manager.
London, King's Cross Station, August, 1873.

Figure 1. Enticing trips for Lincoln excursionists. Advertisements in the *Lincolnshire Chronicle*, 15 August 1873.
From the Local Studies Collection, Lincoln Central Library, by courtesy of Lincolnshire County Council, Education & Cultural Services Directorate.

these resorts were less than two and a half hours journey from Lincoln, making it possible to travel there and back in a day, or sometimes within an afternoon. Other destinations popular with Lincoln trippers in the early days of excursions were London, Manchester (which had the attraction of Belle Vue Pleasure Gardens with their own station nearby), and Chatsworth, just a couple of miles from Rowsley station in Derbyshire. In the late nineteenth century, as the rail network spread, people were able to travel increasingly further afield. From the 1890s it was possible to travel from Lincoln to Blackpool by taking the train to Southport, then catching a steamer across the Ribble Estuary, but it was not until 1905 that a day trip from Lincoln to Blackpool could be taken, when travelling time was five hours each way, allowing just two hours in Blackpool.[13] However, many would take the trip, as a different destination was always a novelty, offering a new experience.

A national event which helped to establish the excursion as a popular pastime was the Great Exhibition, held in Hyde Park, London in 1851. This was well publicised and railway trips were run to the Great Exhibition from all over the country. Lincoln people enjoyed a good deal, as two railway companies were operating services from Lincoln to London at the time. The Great Northern route was quicker, but the Midland route was deemed to be prettier, and offered cheap rates to parties of twelve or more. Competition between the two companies led to such cheap fares that people were travelling to Lincoln from places like Boston and Newark in order to take advantage of the Lincoln fare.[14] Trips ran throughout the summer of 1851, and on one day, Monday, 11 August, 5600 people were reported to have travelled from Lincoln to London to enjoy the Exhibition.[15]

Some of the early excursion trains were very long, and transported large numbers of people – at the time they were often called 'monster trains': in June 1848 over 1000 people went from Lincoln to Derby in a train of 46 carriages, and in 1849 a party of 3000 teetotallers descended on Lincoln in one day.[16] If these numbers are anything to go by, it seems that trippers enjoyed being in large crowds. On Bank Holidays, resorts were packed with visitors: on Monday, 3 August 1863, 30,000 visited Cleethorpes, and on August Bank Holiday Monday 1882, 22,000 day trippers came to Skegness and the shops ran out of food.[17]

As well as being crowded, trips were noisy occasions. Trippers loved to have musical accompaniment, and a large outing, such as a work's annual outing, would often have a brass band playing on the station as it departed. In the case of a children's outing, the young people might be marched to the station in a crocodile, accompanied by a local band, whose members might travel with them, entertaining them with music throughout the day.[18] Those visiting seaside resorts or pleasure gardens, such as Manchester's Belle Vue would be entertained by bands playing along the promenade and in public gardens.[19] While travelling, trippers often joined in communal singing, particularly on the homeward journey, and choir outings would often take the lead in this. In 1904, when the choir of St Andrew's Church were returning from their outing to Scarborough, they sang old English glees (part songs) to the pleasure of their travelling companions. As they had brought sheet music with them, and one choir member had brought a violin, they were obviously anticipating this.[20]

Excursions were crammed with activity. As the opportunity for a day out came infrequently, it was usually spent seeing and doing as much as possible, rather than as a chance for rest and relaxation. Excursions usually departed very early in the morning and returned late at night.[21] During the 1880s, many new facilities were developed at resorts to cater for trippers. Piers were opened at Cleethorpes in 1873 and Skegness in 1881. On payment of an entrance fee, people could walk along them, enjoying the amusements and music there. In 1878, Tower Gardens, with a pavilion, skittle alleys and public conveniences, were opened in Skegness, and by 1882 a trip could be taken round the Wash by steam boat.[22] By the 1890s, donkey rides on the sands were available at most seaside resorts, and switchbacks, swimming baths and boating could all be enjoyed at Skegness.[23] Restaurants were opening up, and although many would take their food with them, the habit of paying to sit down to a 'knife and fork tea' was spreading down the social scale.[24]

As time went on, new forms of transport brought greater flexibility to the excursionists. By the 1880s many working class people could afford a safety bicycle, which was more comfortable and easier to ride than the penny farthing. This opened up the possibility of visiting many pretty villages in the area, including those not on the rail network. By 1895, at least three cycling clubs in Lincoln were organising 'spins' on Saturday afternoons to coincide with the workers' half-holiday.[25] By the beginning of the twentieth century, motorised transport was becoming available to the excursionist. In 1900 charabancs were being advertised for private hire.[26] These

Figure 2. Charabanc outing to a football match outside the *Blue Anchor*, Lincoln High Street. *From the Local Studies Collection, Lincoln Central Library, by courtesy of Lincolnshire County Council, Education & Cultural Services Directorate.*

motorised carriages (see Figure 2), holding around 28 people, appealed to smaller groups who might appreciate greater privacy than the train could offer, opened up new destinations away from the rail network, and in their early days had great novelty value. St Martin's church choirmen had several outings by motor car in the early twentieth century, visiting, among other places, the Dukeries area of Nottinghamshire.[27]

Excursions also provided opportunities for the working classes to spend their increasing leisure time in 'rational or 'improving' ways. Trips could be organised to educational activities, exhibitions, lectures, sports fixtures and places of natural beauty or historic interest. Thomas Cook of Market Harborough, the tour operator and a staunch member of the temperance movement, claimed that excursions promoted 'the expansion of the intellect, the grasping of information... the improvement in health and prospects... with numerous other influences of a happy and beneficial tendency'.[28] The *Lincolnshire Chronicle* endorsed the view that trips were beneficial, noting in 1870 that there was a need for Saturday afternoon excursions for workers and their families, as 'when working men go out by train they more often than not take their wives with them, instead of spending their surplus cash on their own gratification'.[29] Local newspapers also reinforced the moral tone of the outings, particularly in the early days. The *Lincolnshire Chronicle* report of an outing of over 1000 people from Lincoln to a Grand Fete at Derby in 1848 stated that 'the most perfect order prevailed' and 'the smiling faces and respectable appearance of the Lincolners were the subject of general remark among strangers'.[30]

Conversely, excursions could be organised to what were considered 'unrespectable' events, such as horse racing, prize fighting or public executions, where drinking, gambling or brawling might feature in the day's activities. These were the subject of public censure, particularly when there was drunkenness, which was even reported on some trips organised by temperance societies.[31] Newspapers would note bad behaviour by Lincoln trippers, as well as good. The *Lincolnshire Chronicle* reported unfavourably on a group of men who disgraced themselves on a trip to Scarborough in 1850, though what they actually did was not mentioned, perhaps to discourage others from copying them.[32] In 1868 the *Capital Punishment Amendment Act* was passed, ensuring that executions were no longer held in public places, where they had been attracting large crowds of day trippers coming by train and generating a spate of public disorder and petty crime.

By the early twentieth century, clubs, societies, church organisations, political groups, works and professional associations were all organising trips, often annually, for their members, in addition to the public excursions run by the railway companies and commercial tour operators such as Thomas Cook. Excursions were an enjoyable feature of working class life and many people had the opportunity to participate in several trips of various kinds in the course of a year.

On Tuesday, 4 August 1914, the day after August Bank Holiday Monday, when so many would have enjoyed an excursion, Britain declared war. Within a few days the government had taken control of the railways and had suspended all pleasure trips by rail.[33] This effectively put a stop to large scale excursions for six years, although there is evidence that wartime excursions did take place by other means, such as river boats and ferries, but the distances that could be travelled this way were shorter.[34] The rail restrictions remained in force until August 1920, so organised excursions by train did not take place again until well after the end of the First World War.[35]

Works' Outings

There were two kinds of excursions for workers. Firstly, there were outings which were arranged and paid for by employers and secondly, those organised and paid for by the workers themselves. Some employers gave their staff a 'treat', an outing which included a meal and provided an occasion for socialising between management and staff. This might include a formal element, with speeches, toasts and votes of thanks. Although it was a 'holiday', employees would be expected to be on their best behaviour. If the head of a firm had a large garden, he might invite his staff there for an afternoon, providing entertainment, music and tea, perhaps in a marquee. In July 1871, the employees of Ruston and Proctor were invited with their wives and fiancées to the home of Mr and Mrs Joseph Ruston at Washingborough Manor House, travelling by special train from Lincoln. Nine hundred people went, and enjoyed a substantial tea and entertainment including races with prizes. The band of the Royal North Lincolnshire Militia played throughout the proceedings, which ended at 9pm, when hearty cheers were given for Mr Ruston. The employees would have been entertained in the garden, where a large marquee had been erected, and would not have entered the house.[36] Employers liked their generosity to be made known to the general public as it was a way of demonstrating their philanthropy to their staff, for when the staff of Beagles, the grocers, were taken to Cleethorpes in 1900, the local paper reported that 'Councillor Beagle defrayed the cost of absolutely every item... no member of the... company had to pay a single penny'.[37] It was accepted that manual workers lost a day's pay when they took a day off to go on an outing, so when Fred Peel, a city corn merchant, gave his regular employees one day off with pay to take a trip of their choice, instead of organising a works outing, this was reported as a 'real holiday', and viewed as a very generous practice.[38] Some works and professional outings had an educational purpose, such as the trips in 1910 to the Printing and Allied Trades Exhibition in London by the Lincoln Typographical Association, and later that year by the staff of Ruddocks stationers.[39] Similarly, the staff of Lincoln Cooperative Society visited the Cooperative Wholesale Society's boot and shoe factory at Leeds in 1914.[40]

Lincoln's 'Foundry Trips' belonged to a second kind of works outing, being organised entirely by the workers. By 1870 (when around ten per cent of Lincoln's population worked in the city's foundries), staff of more than one factory were organising joint outings for their workmates. When staff from Robey and Co. ran two trips to Scarborough and Cleethorpes on Saturday 16 July, an announcement appeared in the newspaper stating that tickets could be bought from the Trips Committee, suggesting a degree of planning and organisation.[41] The staff of Clayton and Shuttleworth combined with the staff of Ruston and Proctor to organise excursions running to Cleethorpes, Hull, London Manchester and Sheffield, all running on Saturday, 30 July, and with the option of returning the same day or staying for two or three days.[42] By 1875 the habit of taking a trip on the last Saturday in July had become fixed for Lincoln workers and their families, and many of the city's shops and businesses closed on that day to allow their staff to take advantage of the many excursions laid on, as the trips were not restricted to the factory workers – anyone who paid could travel on them.[43] It sometimes happened that the August Bank Holiday Monday fell immediately after Trips Saturday, giving people a three day break, and some excursions were arranged so that trippers could travel outwards on the Saturday, returning home on the Sunday or the Monday (Figure 3). As time went on the 'Trips' break was extended and, by the early 1900s, it had become known as 'Trips Week' as many were taking the whole week off work. In practice, many took just a few days away, spending the rest of the week back in Lincoln, but still off work.[44]

The 'Trips' were organised by a Committee of about a dozen workers from the various foundries, who were allowed certain travel concessions in recognition of this work, but were not paid for it. Well in advance, they would negotiate with the four

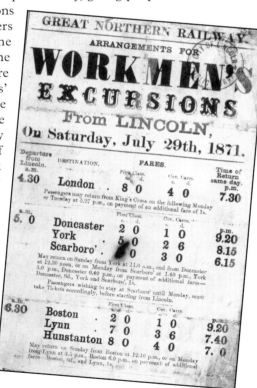

Figure 3. Poster advertising excursions on 'Trips Saturday', 1871.
From the Local Studies Collection, Lincoln Central Library, by courtesy of Lincolnshire County Council, Education & Cultural Services Directorate.

railway companies operating in the city to ensure that the required number of trains would be running to popular destinations, and that fares would be at the cheapest possible price. It was essential that the companies knew the dates well in advance, so that rolling stock could be moved to Lincoln in readiness for the last Saturday in July. The 'Trips' were a big occasion for Lincoln people. The prudent saved throughout the year to pay for their excursions or contributed to a 'club', run by one of the factory foremen.[45] Some put in overtime to earn extra money to go. Others pawned their valuables: Thomas Cooper the Chartist, who lived in Lincoln for some years, wrote in 1885,

> *50 feather beds, pawned by the workers in two days to get the means of having their usual July railway trip! This has just been enacted in the old cathedral city where I am writing.*[46]

When 'Trips Saturday' arrived, packed trains would leave the city, starting at about three o'clock in the morning. By eight o'clock most people had departed. In the early hours of the morning, Lincoln would be crowded with people all dressed in their best clothes for an outing, yet later in the day, when everyone was away, the streets were deserted.[47]

Between 1871 and 1902, local newspapers annually published the numbers of tickets sold from Lincoln to specific destinations on 'Trips Saturday'. In 1871, when Lincoln's population was 26,723, a total of 9783 tickets were sold; the highest number of tickets were sold in 1899 (18,537). This figure dropped sharply in the early 1900s when rail fares increased drastically, so that in 1901, only 9828 tickets were sold to a population of 48,784.[48] In 1875 trips were run to a total of 29 destinations, compared to 88 in 1902. This was chiefly due to the opening up of new stations and destinations between these years, but also because the railway companies were willing to run more trains and permit more stops when more people were travelling. Throughout the period, Grimsby and Cleethorpes remained the most popular destinations, with 2158 visitors in 1875 and 1087 in 1902, while many tickets were also sold to London, Manchester, Sheffield, Scarborough, Hull and Skegness. Mablethorpe, Sutton on Sea and Blackpool, none of which had been accessible by rail in 1871, were among the most popular resorts in 1902. Inland resorts, such as the spa towns of Matlock and Buxton were also popular. Some of the destinations visited in 1902, such as Douglas (Isle of Man) and Llandudno, must have been visited by those staying for one or more nights, as it would have been impossible to travel there and back in a day.[49]

Conclusions

By the eve of the First World War, excursions had become an established leisure activity in Britain, enjoyed by people of all ages and social groups. They catered for a wide range of interests and offered a great variety of destinations and activities to be enjoyed on arrival. Many provided educational opportunities. In the 1840s a railway excursion was a new experience, a rare novelty, which was only just becoming available to Lincoln people. By 1914, many working people were able to afford several outings in the course of a year, and some could afford to stay away for several days. For those who went away more frequently, there was less pressure to rush around seeing and doing as much as possible in the space of a few hours, as was the custom of the Victorian tripper, so excursions could be enjoyed at a more leisurely pace. An article in the *Lincolnshire Chronicle* in 1914, entitled 'Hints to Holidaymakers', advised moderation, warning of the dangers of too much walking, bathing and generally rushing around, and remonstrating against 'the average man' who 'rushed into his holiday like a mad bull tilting into a china shop'.[50] As resorts had been developed over the Victorian period, there were now shops, facilities and more amusements and attractions at the destinations than in the mid nineteenth century. Practices which had once been the preserve of the wealthy, such as eating in a hotel, or travelling by motorised transport, were spreading down the social scale, and becoming accessible to the working classes. However, the development of the excursion was stopped short by the First World War, and large scale organised trips were comparatively rare until the summer of 1920.

Notes and References

1. J W F Hill, *Victorian Lincoln*, Cambridge, 1974, pp.120, 121 and 123.
2. The *Census Reports* give the population of Lincoln as 11,843 in 1831 and 37,313 in 1881.
3. *Census Report* 1871.
4. J Walvin, *Beside the Seaside*, 1978, p.53.
5. E H Hunt, *British Labour History 1815–1914*, 1981, pp.78 –80.
6. J W F Hill, *Victorian Lincoln*, Cambridge, 1974, p.292 and *Lincolnshire Chronicle*, 14 May 1880.
7. E H Hunt, *British Labour History 1815–1914*, 1981, p.73.
8. *Lincolnshire Chronicle*, 7 August 1846.
9. J W F Hill, *Victorian Lincoln*, Cambridge, 1974, p.7.
10. J G Ruddock and R E Pearson, *The Railway History of Lincoln*, 2nd ed., 1985, pp.191 and 116.
11. D N Robinson, *The Book of the Lincolnshire Seaside*, Buckingham, 1981, p.63.
12. R E Pearson, 'Railways in Relation to Resort Development in East Lincolnshire', *East Midlands Geographer*, 4, 1968, pp.281 –294.
13. *Lincolnshire Chronicle*, 15 July 1905.
14. *Lincolnshire Chronicle*, 8 August 1851.
15. *Lincolnshire Chronicle*, 15 August 1851.

16. *Lincolnshire Chronicle*, 30 June 1848 and 29 June 1849.

17. D N Robinson, *Book of the Lincolnshire Seaside*, Buckingham, 1981, p.63 and R Leleux, *A Regional History of the Railways of Great Britain, Volume IX: The East Midlands*, 2nd ed., Newton Abbott, 1984, pp.204-5.

18. *Lincolnshire Chronicle*, 29 June 1849 and 26 August 1853.

19. A Delgado, *The Annual Outing and Other Excursions*, 1977, p.155 and J K Walton, *The English Seaside Resort: A Social History 1750-1914*, Leicester, 1983, p.167.

20. *St Andrew's Parish Magazine*, August 1904.

21. *Lincolnshire Chronicle*, 14 September 1895.

22. D N Robinson, *The Book of the Lincolnshire Seaside*, Buckingham, 1981, pp.99-100 and p.66.

23. *Lincolnshire Chronicle*, 1 June 1895 and 24 August 1895.

24. *Lincolnshire Chronicle*, 6 September 1890 and 31 August 1895.

25. *Lincolnshire Chronicle*, 7 June 1895.

26. *Lincolnshire Chronicle*, 19 May 1900 and 29 June 1900.

27. *St Martin's Parish Magazine*, July 1912.

28. Quoted in J Pudney, *The Thomas Cook Story*, 1953, p.74.

29. *Lincolnshire Chronicle*, 3 June 1870.

30. *Lincolnshire Chronicle*, 30 June 1848.

31. *Lincolnshire Chronicle*, 1 September 1848.

32. *Lincolnshire Chronicle*, 6 September 1850.

33. A Delgado, *The Annual Outing and Other Excursions*, 1977, p.140.

34. *Gainsborough News*, 25 June 1915 and 9 July 1915.

35. A and E Jordan, *Away for the Day: the Railway Excursion in Britain 1830 to the Present Day*, Kettering, 1991, p.247.

36. *Lincolnshire Chronicle*, 28 July 1871.

37. *Lincolnshire Chronicle*, 25 August 1900.

38. *Lincolnshire Chronicle*, 28 July 1900.

39. *Lincolnshire Chronicle*, 30 May 1910 and 10 June 1910.

40. *Lincolnshire Chronicle*, 23 May 1914.

41. *Lincolnshire Chronicle*, 8 July 1870.

42. *Lincolnshire Chronicle*, 15 July 1870.

43. *Lincolnshire Chronicle*, 6 August 1875.

44. *Lincolnshire Chronicle*, 29 July 1910. Often sporting events and village shows took place in and around Lincoln during 'Trips Week' from mid week onwards (e.g., *Lincolnshire Chronicle*, 27 July 1910) suggesting that people would be off work, but in Lincoln.

45. *Lincolnshire Chronicle*, 19 July 1930.

46. T Cooper, *Thoughts at Four Score*, 1885, pp.31-32.

47. *Lincolnshire Chronicle*, 6 August 1875.

48. *Lincolnshire Chronicle*, 2 August 1902. It is not known how many tickets were sold to Lincoln people and how many to those who came in from the surrounding villages, but it is likely that the majority went to Lincoln workers and their families.

49. *Lincolnshire Chronicle*, 6 August 1875 and 2 August 1902.

50. *Lincolnshire Chronicle*, 17 July 1914.

Acknowledgements

I would like to thank Dr J A Johnston for help and encouragement with this project and Mr J S English and Pat Gregory for drawing my attention to some helpful references.

12. Lincoln's Cinemas in the Twentieth Century

by George Clarke

THROUGHOUT MUCH OF THE TWENTIETH CENTURY, cinema-going proved a popular pastime in Lincoln. By the end of the 1930s, Lincoln had as many as eight venues equipped to screen films. Undoubtedly, cinema-going was at its height during the 1930s and 1940s. In 1940, annual admissions to films in Britain totalled 1,027 million.[1] Various surveys of cinema-going were conducted during the 1930s. It seemed that about 40 per cent of the total population went to the cinema in any one week and, of these, about two-thirds went twice weekly or more.[2] As J B Priestley noted in 1933, the cultural life of Britain's towns and cities was in danger of becoming nothing 'but films, films, films.'[3] This article looks specifically at the varied venues in which Lincoln's filmgoers were able to satisfy their craving for celluloid.

The early exhibition of films in Lincoln

A variety of venues in Lincoln offered audiences the opportunity to see moving pictures in the early years of the twentieth century. The first films screened in Lincoln were, as in most towns, shown in booths at local fairs. In the final years of the nineteenth century, a Boston-based showman, George Howden included a bioscope show amongst his fairground attractions. The bioscope was an early means by which moving pictures were brought to a paying audience. Howden's fairground rides visited Lincoln regularly during the period. Consequently, it is fair to assume that Howden brought his bioscope show to the city. The equipment used by these cinema pioneers was cumbersome. Film widths varied from 40mm to 75mm, with 35mm finally becoming the standard width. With a running speed of 16 frames per second, films of 75m (250 feet) in length lasted about a minute on screen.

In 1909, Lincoln's first cinema opened its doors, though its hours of business were restricted. St Hugh's Hall on Monks Road ran hourly shows on Saturdays between 2pm and 9pm using portable equipment. Admission prices ranged between 2d and 4d. This building is still standing and is used as a Parish Hall.

Films at the Theatre Royal, Clasketgate

Between 1909 and 1913, a limited company called Cinematograph Film Makers and Exhibitors Film Exchange operated from 248 High Street. This company rented and distributed films, though it seems to have enjoyed only moderate success. The London Bioscope Company, by contrast, was more successful. It screened films in Lincoln at the Theatre Royal in a series of summer seasons during the second decade of the century (Figure 1). In May 1913, for instance, its programme of films included *The King's Service, The Spring of Life, Training a Tight Wad, and Flash of Lightning*. These films ran for three days when they were replaced by a completely different programme. One of the first colour films, made using a process called 'Kinemacolor', was shown at the Theatre Royal in June 1913 as part of the theatre's summer film programme.

Theatres such as the Theatre Royal played an important role in enabling early films to be shown at a time when tailor-made venues for film were rare. Undoubtedly, in the short-term, such theatres benefited from the additional revenues brought in by this pioneering breed of filmgoers. In the longer term, however, it is possible that, eventually, those who had their appetite for film whetted in theatres ultimately deserted live performances, preferring instead the purpose-built 'picture theatre' to the 'proper theatre'.[4] Towards the end of the century, the Theatre Royal, for a short period, doubled as both a 'proper theatre' and a 'picture theatre'. In February 1985, moves were made to install a new projection room and equip it with the latest projection equipment. This was in order to screen special interest films, mostly on Sundays, with children's shows on Saturday mornings. The first of these special shows took place on 31 March 1987, when an archive film, *Sixty Years of Aircraft*, was shown. This was followed in June by a special screening of *The Wild and the*

Figure 1a, b and c. Early film programme posters from the Theatre Royal, 1912 and 1913. *Author's collection.*

Willing, a film shot in and around Lincoln. An experimental season of current releases was tried in 1989, but has not been repeated since.

The Central Cinema, St Swithin's Square, 1902–1944

Another early venue for the screening of films in Lincoln was provided at the New Central Hall. This opened on 20 October 1902 as a centre for temperance activities. It was designed by Will Mortimer and arranged in the style of a modern theatre. It accommodated 1560 people. As temperance activities declined in popularity, New Central Hall's proprietor, Will Gadsby, increasingly turned to the screening of films as a means of revenue raising. Arthur H Vidler introduced the film *A Christmas Dream* on the 'Electro Chrono Bioscope' during the 1904 pantomime season. Within a short space of time, the venue was converted into a permanent picture house. It boasted 'flicker-free and rock-steady pictures' (Figure 2).

The Central Cinema, as it became known, was maintained to a high standard, and can be regarded as one of Lincoln's premier picture palaces during its life. Upon acquisition by Central Picture

Figure 2. Central Cinema, exterior, c1938. *From the Local Studies Collection, Lincoln Central Library, by courtesy of Lincolnshire County Council, Education and Cultural Services Directorate.*

Theatre Ltd, a firm owned by Leeds-based Jack, Oscar, Gerald and Sydney Segelman, a complete interior refurbishment was undertaken. State of the art projection equipment was installed, as well as a Western Electric Wide Range sound system. Entrance to the stalls was through swing doors and a curtain, which kept out unwanted daylight. Patrons were shown to their seats by torch-waving usherettes. In order to reach the circle, visitors did an about turn at the paybox and followed the stairs in the foyer to the circle lounge, about halfway up the building. Here, well-upholstered seats were available in which to relax before entering the auditorium itself. The circle was very steep, but this did allow a full and unrestricted view of the stage and screen. The circle was particularly popular amongst members of the younger generation who made good use of the double seating arrangements.

In 1944, a second-hand 2/6 Christie pipe organ was installed. However, before it made its debut, on the night of 6/7 March the entire cinema was gutted by a fire, which was started by an arsonist. The fire caused damage estimated between £15,000 and £20,000. The Central Cinema was never rebuilt and remained in ruins until its final demolition in March 1960, when Thorngate House was built on the site.

The Cinematograph Hall/Exchange Kinema/Astoria, Cornhill, 1910–1956

This was another of Lincoln's cinemas which had not been built specifically to screen films. The building was originally used as a corn exchange, following its opening in 1879. The first cinema in Lincoln was housed in the building. This opened on 28 May 1910 as the Cinematograph Hall. In 1912, John Gale and Company Limited took over the operation. As cinema became established within Britain, ownership of chains of cinemas became increasingly common. John Gale and Company Limited owned cinemas in Gainsborough and Canning Town. The company also took over leases relating to premises at Darlington, Grantham, Lowestoft, Newark Peterborough and Worcester, as well as in Lincoln (Figure 3).

In March 1928, the premises

Figure 3. Advertisement for *The Gold Rush*, showing at the Corn Exchange, March 1926. *Author's collection.*

Figure 4. Staff of the Exchange Cinema, 16 May 1932.
Back row (left to right): Len Codling, projectionist; Mrs Carter, cashier; Mr Rolleston, projectionist. Front row, (left to right) Three unknown usherettes; Arthur Thomas, chief projectionist; Mr B Harris, manager; Mrs Harris, assistant manager; unknown doorman; two unknown usherettes.
Author's collection.

were taken over by Denman/Gaumont, a larger chain of cinema-owners. The cinema was renamed the Exchange Kinema, and quickly became known locally as the 'Ekky'. Throughout much of its existence, the Exchange Kinema occupied a relatively lowly place in Lincoln's cinema hierarchy. Seating was basic and, being on a flat floor, patrons were always anxious about the size of those sitting immediately in front of them. On Thursday nights, the cinema's seating had to be removed to make way for the Friday corn market, before being speedily replaced in time for the evening show. Its staple fare comprised westerns and serials until the postwar years, when an increasingly sophisticated cinema audience demanded musicals and dramas (Figure 4).

In April 1954, Central Picture Theatres, owners of Central

Figure 5. *Astoria* Cinema, in use as a bingo hall, 1972. *Author's collection.*

Cinema, bought the Exchange Kinema and refurbished it extensively. In November 1954, the cinema reopened as the Astoria. Just over a year later, in January 1956, the Rank Organisation took control and closed it in June 1956. It was transformed into a roller rink in 1957, and, in 1972, like many former cinemas, it became a bingo hall (Figure 5). Since the early 1980s, the building has been used as a retail outlet, firstly as a fast-food restaurant and, more recently, as a Co-operative store.

The Grand Theatre, High Street, 1911-1960

Arthur Vidler, who had previously screened films at the Central Cinema, bought Garmston House, an eighteenth century building, in 1911 and opened it as the Lincoln Theatre (Figure 6). This was the second full-time cinema to open in the city. The house was converted into a vestibule, projection room and a manager's office. An auditorium was built at the back of the house, extending to Hungate, which accommodated 930 patrons on a flat floor.

In 1913, the cinema was renamed the Grand Electric. Under the proprietorship of Vidler and Will Gadsby, who had also been involved in the managing of the Central Cinema, the Grand screened the first film combined with sound in Lincoln. This was screened as early as 1913 and was entitled *Living Pictures and Living Voices*. The first 'talkie' shown in Lincoln was *Showboat*, starring Paul Robeson. This opened on 23 September 1929 (Figure 7).

In 1937, the dominant cinema company in Lincoln, Central Picture Theatres Limited, gained control of the Grand Cinema. In keeping with other cinemas owned by the group, a Western Electric 'Wide Range' sound system was installed (Figure 8). In an industry characterised by rapid change, as has been revealed here already, it is

Figure 6. (left) The Grand Cinema. Exterior prior to opening in 1911. *Author's collection.*

Figure 7. The Grand Cinema. Exterior c.1929. *Author's collection.*

CONTROLLING · CENTRAL LINCOLN · RITZ LINCOLN · GRAND LINCOLN · PLAZA LINCOLN · EXCHANGE LINCOLN · FORUM LEEDS
ASSOCIATED COMPANIES CONTROLLING: CENTRAL HARROGATE · EMPIRE NORMANTON · GRAND NORMANTON · REGAL ECCLESHILL, BRADFORD
GREENGATES BRADFORD · EMPIRE RAWDON · PLAZA BATLEY · PICTURE HOUSE WOODLANDS, DONCASTER · MELBOURNE LEICESTER

CENTRAL PICTURE THEATRES (LINCOLN) LTD

**YORKS AND LINCS
PICTURE HOUSES LTD**

HEAD OFFICE:
CENTRAL CHAMBERS
41 ALBION STREET, LEEDS 1
TEL · LEEDS 26910 Sept.9th 1941

SOUND BY WESTERN ELECTRIC

Figure 8. Letter head for Central Picture Theatres (Lincoln) Ltd, 1941. *Author's collection.*

noteworthy that Douglas Clark was appointed manager of the Grand in 1939 and retained the post until the cinema's closure on 21 February 1960.

The cinema's closure was enforced. A proposed road was to cut across the site. However, it was never built. The former cinema was bought by the Freemasons, and subsequently sold to the city council. For some years it was used by a local firm for storage. The building suffered a lengthy period of general neglect. In July 1986, it was demolished (Figure 9).

Figure 9. The Grand Cinema. Derelict stage and proscenium, c1976. *Author's collection.*

Despite its name, the Grand never achieved much status. Although it showed many first-run films, often signifying a cinema of high standing, the Grand's inferior seating accommodation meant it was never amongst the highest ranks of the city's cinema hierarchy.

The Picture House/Regal Cinema, High Street, 1915-1966

The Lincoln Picture House was purpose-built for its owners by a Lincoln building contractor, Arthur Rix.

Upon construction, the Picture House was Lincoln's most 'state of the art' cinema. Admission prices at the higher end of the tariff range reflected its high position in the cinema hierarchy. Whilst seats could be secured for 3d and 6d, the most expensive seats could cost 9d.

The Picture House was bought by Associated British Cinemas,

Figure 10. The Regal Cinema, 217/8 High Street, c.1960.
Author's collection.

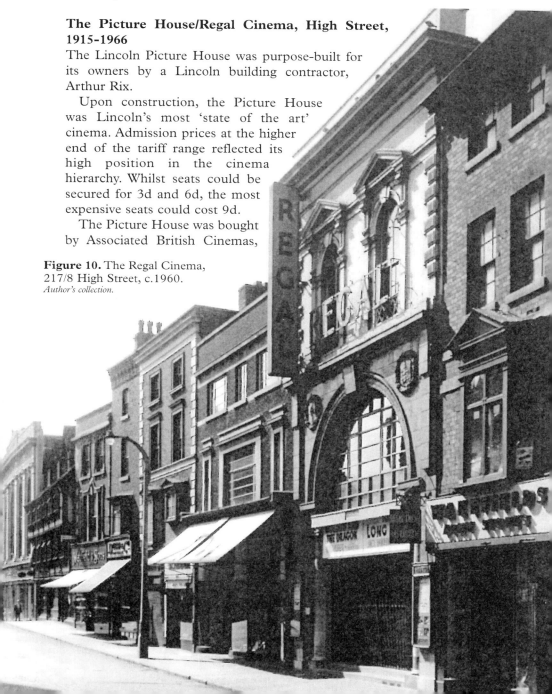

Figure 11. The Regal Cinema. Interior, 1966. *Author's collection.*

(ABC) in 1930 and extensively refurbished. Amidst some ceremony – including the presence of the film star Dodo Watts – the cinema was reopened as the Regal on 12 January 1931.

The first film shown at the Regal starred Conrad Nagel in *A Lady Surrenders*. The Regal was well maintained and enjoyed substantial investment by ABC. A Western Electric sound system was installed in

Figure 12. The Regal Cinema. Projectionist Sid Whitelam and manager, Mr Ritter, in the box before the final performance of *Mary Poppins*, February 1966. *Author's collection.*

1931 and, in 1955, Cinemascope was introduced.

The first Cinemascope film screened at the cinema was the spectacular musical *Seven Brides for Seven Brothers* (Figure 10).

The Regal, once a very popular cinema in the city, entertained cinema-goers for 51 years. It screened many first-run films, but, it was upstaged in 1936, when ABC also opened the Savoy Cinema in the city. From then onwards, it was destined to play second to the Savoy in its choice of films on the ABC circuit.

In its early days, the Regal was not regarded very highly by many cinema-goers because of its poor acoustics. However, these problems were overcome in later years as sound systems improved and the building was refurbished.

In its heyday, the Regal was rated about third in Lincoln's cinema popularity stakes (Figure 11). Its proximity to the river occasionally caused problems, though, as it was not unknown for the odd rat to

Figure 13. The Regal Cinema. Demolition in progress. Looking towards the rear stalls and circle. *Author's collection.*

make an unwelcome appearance in the auditorium!

The Regal closed in February 1966. Its final film screened was *Mary Poppins*. After a week's record business, Mary Poppins left the building and the cinema was demolished. The Littlewoods store now occupies the site (Figures 12 and 13).

Empire Music Hall/Palace Theatre/Plaza Cinema, Newland, 1901-1943

In 1871, the Lincoln Freemasons bought part of a private garden in Newland in order to build a meeting place. A hall was built in a Gothic style, designed by a local architect, William Watkins. It was used for public entertainment and seated up to 1500. Two brothers, F and A Conlon bought the premises and staged shows there, whilst the Freemasons rented the front section of the building until they moved to Guildhall Street and, later, to Mint Street.

In 1901, the Empire was bought by a local grocer and city councillor, George H Beadle, who opened a music hall in the premises. His pricing strategy sought to attract a high class audience. Best seats in the stalls cost 1s 2d and seats in the balcony and side galleries were priced at 1s 3d. The venture lasted barely three months, though his expensive red velvet curtains, with his initials emblazoned in gold, lasted the life of the theatre!

The theatre was bought by the Sheffield-based theatrical entrepreneur Frank McNaghten, who reopened it on 6 January 1902

as the Palace theatre. Vaudeville acts were booked regularly. In 1918, the Palace played host to the young Gracie Fields, in a revue called *It's a Bargain*. Many other well known names graced the boards of the Palace, including Harry Tate and George Formby. Often, the show would be preceded by a newsreel. During the 1920s, audiences dwindled, largely as a consequence of the rise of cinema. The Palace Theatre closed its doors on 17 May 1930.

Like many other music halls, the Palace was bought by a cinema chain (Figure 14). 'Picture theatre' was replacing 'proper theatre'.

Figure 14. The Palace Theatre. Exterior, c.1930. *Author's collection.*

More precisely, Central Picture Theatres bought the Palace Theatre and reopened it as the Plaza Cinema in 1931. With a seating capacity of 1247, the Plaza screened popular films throughout the 1930s heyday of cinema. However, on 23 May 1943, a mystery fire destroyed the building and killed a nightwatchman. Many rumours spread regarding the cause of the blaze. These ranged from a burning cigarette to an incendiary bomb. The mystery was never solved.

Owing to wartime restrictions, rebuilding was not possible. The Plaza was finally demolished in 1953. The Plaza lay bottom of Lincoln's cinema popularity list. Seating arrangements were uncomfortable, the auditorium was invariably cold and, in this adapted building, the sound never did justice to the films screened.

Savoy/ABC/Cannon, Saltergate, 1936-1988

The Savoy was Lincoln's premier cinema. It was built on a site of a number of houses, a printing works and a bottle factory. It was a purpose-built cinema, which was designed by a London-based architect, William R Glen and constructed by the Lincoln firm of William Wright and Son. Its owner was Associated British Cinemas Ltd, which already had a stake in Lincoln's cinema industry as it possessed the Regal. As befitted a splendid picture palace, the Savoy opened amidst much pomp and pageantry (Figure 15). The cinema

Figure 15. Savoy Cinema. Interior in 1936. *Author's collection.*

Figure 16. Savoy Cinema. Exterior view, showing the familiar 'ABC' triangle and the original frontage, c1949. *Author's collection.*

Figure 17. Savoy Cinema. Projection room, with Ross FC projectors and Western Electric Wide Range sound equipment, 1936. *Author's collection.*

was opened on 14 December 1936 by the Mayor of Lincoln, J E Fordham. After the cinema organ, a six rank Compton, with melotone, was put through its paces by ABC's premier organist, Wilfred Southworth, who played at many ABC openings, speeches were made by the mayor and the Chairman of ABC, A S Moss. The inaugural film, *A Tale of Two Cities*, was shown to a near capacity audience (Figures 16 and 17).

The Savoy name was dropped in April 1961, when the cinema took the name of the company which owned it – ABC. Throughout the first 36 years of its operation, the cinema provided a first class auditorium, which was used not only for cinema presentations but also for a variety of other events, ranging from pop concerts to carol singing. However, in retrospect, the cinema, and Lincoln itself, was dealt a blow by extensive alterations which

Figure 18. The Cannon Cinema. Co-habiting with bingo, c1987. *Author's collection.*

Figure 19. Rear view of the Cannon Cinema from the Waterside, c1986.
Author's collection.

took place to the cinema during June 1972. The auditorium was significantly reduced in size to form a 549 seater cinema. Bingo was now provided in the former stalls area (Figure 18). The cinema reopened in August 1972, with Frankie Howard in *Up Front*. The 'improvements' were severely criticised by cinema-goers. As a consequence of the changes, the auditorium's acoustics deteriorated considerably. A High Frequency (HF) speaker had been removed

Figure 20. The Cannon Cinema. The stage under demolition, 1990.
Author's collection.

and smaller speaker units installed. However, these were unable to disperse upper frequency sounds to parts of the circle, which the old HF unit used to do. The problem was rectified by the experienced ABC area engineer, Bill Croft, who had anticipated the difficulties. He obtained an old HF unit from a closed cinema and installed it in the new auditorium. 'I told them', said Bill, 'but they wouldn't bloody listen.'

In September 1983, ABC announced a £100,000 facelift for the cinema. This was to include new carpets, seats, a partial redecoration and the installation of Dolby Stereo sound. Screen tabs were also to be fitted. The circle cinema had never had them. From 27 October 1983, curtains once again opened at the start of a performance. Unfortunately, though, these had a significantly shorter lifespan than those of the Plaza.

On 15 November 1986, ownership of ABC's cinemas across Britain was transferred to the Cannon Group (Figure 19). In October 1988, Cannon sold its Lincoln cinema to Pembroke Developments. The cinema was closed to make way for a new retail centre. The final film shown at the cinema starred Barry Humphries in *Les Patterson Saves the World*. Unfortunately, Australia's most famous cultural attaché was unable to save the Savoy from closure (Figure 20).

The Ritz/Odeon, High Street, 1937-1981; 1985-1997

The Ritz was, like the Savoy, a 'super cinema' built to accommodate the burgeoning numbers of film enthusiasts who flocked to movies during the 1930s. It was built on a site adjoining St Marks railway station. Its auditorium could seat 1600 people. The cinema was built from plans drawn up by the city council architect, Leslie Norton and was built by a London firm of contractors for the owners Central Picture Theatres Ltd. Most of Lincoln's cinemas by the Second World War were controlled by this Leeds-based company, as the company's letter head makes clear.

During its construction, the Ritz was plagued by a series of setbacks, including accidents and material shortages. Consequently, it was 27 weeks in construction and failed in its attempt to open before its principal rival, the Savoy, which was owned by ABC. Indeed, when the cinema was opened on 22 February 1937, development work was still in progress. Adjustments to the projector were made during the opening of the film *San Francisco*, which starred Clark Gable and Jeanette McDonald. Most of the audience probably thought that these adjustments were all part of the picture's

Figure 21. Odeon Cinema, (formerly the Ritz), July 1970. *Author's collection.*

earthquake sequence!

Like the Savoy, the Ritz was technologically at the forefront of Lincoln's cinema provision. It was the first cinema in the country to use the Western Electric Mirrorphonic Sound System. This enabled the hard of hearing to plug into deaf aid sets at the back of the seats. In 1954, the Ritz screened the first Cinemascope presentation in the city, when it showed *The Robe*, produced by 20th Century Fox on a 40ft x 20ft screen. The introduction of this new technology helped to boost box office takings at a time when cinema attendances were falling off badly following the emergence of popular television. The decline in cinema-going caused a significant shake-up in the industry. The Ritz was taken over by the Rank Organisation in 1954 and it was renamed the Odeon (Figures 21 and 22). Rank closed the

Figure 22. Odeon Cinema, (formerly the Ritz). Interior lights as in 1970. Trough indirect light reinstated, 1991. *Author's collection.*

Figure 23. The Ritz in its heyday. An oil painting by the author's son, Stephen Clarke. A copy of the painting was sent to the owner of the *Ritz*, Barry Stead, upon its reopening as part of a successful campaign to reinstate the cinema's neon lighting. *Stephen Clarke.*

Odeon in October 1981.

In October 1984, a sale was agreed with Barry Stead, a director of the Royal Centre in Nottingham. The cinema was substantially refurbished and reopened as the Ritz Theatre. The Odeon's projectors, which had been carefully mothballed by the former chief projectionist, Eric Williamson, were once more in use on 15 February 1985 when the Ritz Theatre screened its first film, *101*

Figure 24. The Ritz. Neon lighting restored! *Author's collection.*

Dalmations to a capacity audience (Figures 23 and 24).

Like the Savoy/ABC, the Ritz sought to extend its revenues through the staging of live performances, such as variety shows and orchestral concerts. Some fifty years earlier, 'proper theatres' sought to supplement box office takings by offering occasional film presentations. Now the cinemas were trying to maximise income by doubling as 'proper theatres' at a time when cinema audiences appeared to be in terminal decline. Despite the big name variety stars, it became apparent that a 1600 seater auditorium was not a viable proposition. In 1994, it was announced that the cinema would close at the end of the year for major alterations. It reopened in May 1995 as the Ritz Film Centre. The large single auditorium was replaced by, initially, two screens and then, later, three screens.

The Ritz Film Centre was much criticised. Many patrons disliked the mini screen system, which, devalued the cinema-going experience. It also meant the loss of a much-valued, albeit unprofitable, live venue. Even with the addition of the spectacular neon lighting, which enhanced the night-time exterior, it became apparent that the Ritz's future was under threat. It was unable to compete with the purpose-built Odeon multiplex, which opened in 1995 on Valentine Road. In December 1997, the closure of the Ritz was announced. Its premises were converted into a bar and restaurant.

The Ritz had served as Lincoln's second largest cinema venue for much of its history and was held in high esteem by cinema-goers. Its war-time service was particularly worthy of mention, especially its circle café which continued to provide meals through difficult times. The Ritz's marketing and publicity was also highly inventive. On one occasion, it had a spitfire plane suspended from the side of the building as part of its marketing of a current release.

Radion Cinema, Newport, 1939-1960

This was the last of Lincoln's inter-war cinemas to be built. It was unusual in that it was located in a suburban area, near Newport Arch in the uphill area of the city. The cinema was opened on 27 March 1939 by the Mayor of Lincoln, Cllr H Wilcock, JP. The Radion's first film programme was characteristic of many of Lincoln's inter-war film presentations comprising a 'B' movie, a newsreel presentation and a main feature. *We're Going to be Rich*, starring Gracie Fields, was the cinema's first main feature. Unfortunately, the outbreak of war in September 1939 meant that the Radion was not going to make anyone rich in its first year of operation. The Radion was requisitioned by the military for the duration of the war and was used

Figure 25. The Radion Cinema before restoration of the neon lighting in 1949. *Author's collection.*

as a base for the Pioneer Corps.

Once the war had ended, much work was needed by the Radion's new owners, Emery Cinema Circuit Ltd of Fylde, in order to re-establish the building as a cinema. The interior was redecorated in similar colours to the original paintwork. The house tabs were replaced, together with a set of screen tabs made from barrage balloon material. These reacted brilliantly to coloured lighting. The cinema's seating capacity was reduced from 850 to 782. This allowed more generous legroom and arguably made the Radion's auditorium

Figure 26. The Radion Cinema. Proscenium and stage, c1949. *Author's collection.*

Figure 27. Radion Cinema. The final show, 1960. *Author's collection.*

the most spacious cinema in town. The cinema was reopened on 4 August 1947, with Mr R G Ascot as manager and Mr Dennis Walls as general circuit manager (Figures 25 and 26).

In the roof void, covered in layers of dust, were the remains of the original neon lighting, which had been stored since the cinema closed upon the declaration of war. After the war, this was carefully removed, cleaned and tested. The lighting was found to be in 90 per cent working order. The remaining pieces were regassed and all of the lighting was refitted to the exterior of the building. This returned the façade of the building to its original state. This neon lighting remained in use until the closure of the cinema in 1960. By this date, it was the only cinema in Lincoln still employing its own neon lighting.

During the 1950s, the Radion proved a popular venue in which to see films. It was refurbished throughout. New projectors and a new sound system were installed during the decade, under the management of Herbert Walls. The Radion catered particularly for its local, suburban market. It showed mainly family films. Although many of its films were running in the city for a second time, this did not seem to have a negative effect upon box office returns. Many cinema-goers waited for a film to be shown at the Radion before seeing it. This enabled them to view the film both in better comfort and for a more modest price than was the case if they had seen the film at its first screening in one of the city's more prestigious cinemas. However, the Radion, like many suburban cinemas, suffered with the emergence of popular television. It screened its last film –*The Five Pennies*, starring Danny Kaye – on 16 July 1960 (Figure 27). The titles of the Radion's first feature film- *We're Going to be Rich* - and its final one demonstrate clearly how experience doesn't always match up to expectation!

I worked at the Radion Cinema from 1948 until its closure in 1960. As I pressed the button to close the tabs for the very last time, I wondered what would become of the building once all the signs of its former life had been extinguished. Finally, it was good news when I heard that BBC Radio Lincolnshire was to occupy the building. It was reassuring to know that the premises were again to be used in the field of entertainment (Figure 28).

Figure 28. The former Radion Cinema. Since 1980, the building has housed BBC Radio Lincolnshire. *Author's collection.*

I have been asked by many people if the building was haunted, as a number of staff have experienced some unexplained 'happenings'. Having spent many nights in the building, working both upstairs in the 'box' or on stage at all hours, I can reveal that I experienced cold spots on stage, which I didn't think anything of at the time. I also understand that someone reported seeing what was thought to be a ghostly lady on the stage area. Perhaps the staff who reported these incidents were right about the ghostly presence. If so, I am sure that she is friendly!

Concluding remarks

Lincoln's cinema history in the twentieth century echoes that of many other towns. It is a story of constant ebb and flow. Initially, existing buildings were converted to the needs of the exciting new leisure pursuit of cinema-going, which enabled so many people to indulge in escapism without leaving their home towns.

During the 1930s, the heyday of the movies, several imposing, purpose-built cinemas were constructed in the town, reflecting the confidence and revenue-raising potential of this leisure industry. Within Lincoln, a clear cinema hierarchy had emerged before the outbreak of the Second World War. At the more prestigious, 'picture palace' end of Lincoln's cinema provision were concerns such as the Savoy and the Ritz; at the other end of the spectrum were cinemas such as the Plaza and the 'Ekky'. Undoubtedly, however, all gave their patrons much pleasure.

Following the war, when alternative forms of entertainment began to emerge, most significantly, popular television, Lincoln's cinemas came under severe threat. As has been shown, a variety of strategies were adopted to stave off financial difficulties: a number of cinemas were 'twinned' and eventually converted to three screens; and some sought to offer live acts as well as recorded ones. Unfortunately, most of these strategies were unsuccessful. Consequently, very few of Lincoln's twentieth-century city centre cinemas have survived.

In recent years, however, cinema-going has begun to rise substantially in popularity, especially amongst the young. Lincoln's sole commercial cinema operator, the Odeon chain, has recently sunk an estimated £11 million into the development of its new 2000 seater, nine-screen multiplex on Brayford Pool.[4] It will be interesting to see whether its life span exceeds that of Lincoln's longest lived purpose-built picture palaces, the Ritz and the Savoy, which both served the city's filmgoers for over half of the twentieth century.

Appendix

The twentieth century cinemas of Lincoln		
Date of opening/first film screening	**Name of Venue**	**Date of closure/last film screening**
1902	Central Hall	1909?
1909	St Hugh's Picture Hall, (Monks Road)	Not known
1909	Central Cinema, (St Swithin's Square)	1944
1910	Cinema Hall/Exchange/Astoria, (Cornhill)	1956
1911	Lincoln Theatre/Grand Cinema, (High Street)	1960
1912 ?	Theatre Royal, (Clasketgate)	
1915	The Picture House/Regal Cinema, (High Street)	1966
1931	The Palace Theatre/Plaza Cinema, (Newland)	1943
1936	Savoy/ABC/Cannon, (Saltergate)	1988
1937	Ritz/Odeon, (High Street)	1981
1939	Radion, (Newport)	1939
1947	Radion, (Newport)	1960
1985	Ritz, (High Street)	1998
1995	Odeon Multiplex, (Valentine Road)	

Notes and References

1. J Richards, *The Age of the Dream Palace*, London, 1984, p.11.
2. J Richards, *The Age of the Dream Palace*, London, 1984, p.12
3. J B Priestley, *An English Journey, London*, 1934, p.121.
4. *Lincolnshire Echo*, 11 April 2000.

A complete bibliography of all the works consulted for this study would be too extensive to print here. Amongst the primary printed sources used in this study were the following:

The Abell Collection, Lincoln Central Library
Lincolnshire Review, 1922-1923
Lincolnshire Life, March 1974
The Stage, 1912
Lincolnshire Echo
Lincolnshire Free Press
Lincolnshire Standard
Kelly's Directory of Lincoln, 1909-1937
Kine Year Books

Acknowledgements

The author wishes to express his sincere appreciation and acknowledgement to the following individuals: Sydney Donaldson, John East, Peter Grey, Brian Hornsey and Peter Washburn. He apologises in advance for any unintentional omissions.

CONTRIBUTORS

INTRODUCTION

Andrew Walker has worked at the University of Lincolnshire and Humberside, where he teaches History, since 1992. He studied as an undergraduate at the University of Manchester, where he obtained a degree in History and then a PGCE. He gained an MA in Local History, Literature and Cultural Tradition from the University of Sheffield in 1989 and went on to obtain a doctorate there in 1994. His PhD examined the social and cultural development of the South Yorkshire coalfield in the second half of the nineteenth century. He has published a number of articles examining the impact of industrialisation upon communities, including a chapter in *Aspects of Sheffield 2*. More recently, he has undertaken research into the early years of the Lincolnshire Show and hopes to publish work on the subject in the near future.

1. DARK SKIES: ROYAL AIR FORCE COMMAND IN LINCOLNSHIRE

Dr Philip Swan has taught History at the University of Lincolnshire and Humberside since 1980. Now a Principal Lecturer in the Department of Journalism and Humanities he is based at the Lincoln campus.

Originally from the West Riding he has lived in North Lincolnshire for the past fourteen years. His research interests include the social history of medicine, regional and local history, and more recently aviation heritage. Between 1988 and January 2001 he was the Director of the EC funded Lincolnshire Aviation Heritage Multimedia Project.

Dr Swan is the editor of the *Journal of Regional and Local Studies* and is a member of a number of committees relating to history and archaeology in Lincolnshire.

2. REMEMBERING THOSE IN LINCOLN'S PRISONS, 1774-1872

Terry Nowell is a Superintendent Methodist Minister in Lincoln, having worked for the Methodist Church since 1970. He studied for a degree in theology at Manchester and obtained a Master of Theology degree from the University of Sheffield. He is at present completing a doctorate at the University of Lincolnshire and Humberside on the role of the prison chaplain, with special reference to  Lincoln. He then hopes to write a novel about some of the characters he has unearthed during his research on prisons.

3. LINCOLN'S TOWN CRIER

Jenny Walton was born and bred in South Wales but has lived in Lincolnshire for almost forty years. She is married with three children and two step-children, all adult, who regularly produce grandchildren. There are nine up to now! Her other great loves in her life are her four large dogs and three cats; she also loves music, especially choral singing. She also performs and directs in amateur theatricals.
Jenny has worked as a writer/editor for a number of business publications, an East Yorkshire paper, and editor for *Lincolnshire Life* magazine. She writes articles for various specialist magazines, both regional and national, and researches and writes scripts for documentary videos that sell worldwide. Her current projects include editing *Aspects of the North Lincolnshire Coast* for Wharncliffe Books and the biography of Joe Frater, a Grimsby-based boxing promoter.

4. GETTING DRUNK IN SEVENTEENTH CENTURY LINCOLN

Jim Johnston was a teacher before he became a Lecturer in History at Sheffield Training College and Worcester College of Education. He then became the Vice Principal of Bishop

Grosseteste College in Lincoln.

At Lincoln, he taught certificate and degree courses in local and regional history for the universities of Hull and Nottingham

5. VISUALISING LINCOLN, THE WORK OF PETER DE WINT

John Sanders was educated at Queen Elizabeth's Grammar School, Horncastle and went on to study history at the University of Nottingham, followed by social work at the University of York.

He has worked in the Lincoln area for over twenty years, and is currently Students' Union General Manager at North Lincolnshire College. During this time he has also studied part-time gaining an MA in Local History, Literature and Cultural Tradition in 1991 from the University of Sheffield, (specialising in Shelley), followed by an MPhil in English Literature in 1997. His thesis was a reassessment of the existentialism of Joseph Conrad. He has long been an admirer of the work of Peter De Wint, and soon hopes to complete a fuller study about the nature of his Romanticism.

6. 'A CITIZEN OF NO MEAN CITY'. EMILY GILBERT 1872-1959: MOTORING PIONEER AND FIRST WOMAN SHERIFF OF LINCOLN

Alice Rodgers was born and brought up in Burton upon Trent, but she has spent the greater part of her adult life in South Yorkshire. Family connections mean that, since her earliest childhood, she has been a regular visitor to Lincoln, the city she loves above all others.

A keen local historian, Alice has contributed articles on topics as varied as mills and wills to the Rotherham and Doncaster volumes of the *Aspects* series.

Originally a teacher, she now divides her time between a part-time job in further education, research, writing and voluntary work in a country house archive.

She is married to a teacher, has two grown-up children and now lives in Maltby, near Rotherham.

7. THE MIDDLE CLASSES IN VICTORIAN LINCOLN

Kate Hill has taught History at the University of Lincolnshire and Humberside since 1995. Her PhD, awarded by the University of Lancaster in 1997, was on British museums and the middle classes in the nineteenth century. She has published on various aspects of the British middle classes' cultural life in the Victorian period, and is currently working on a book about the establishment and growth of municipal museums.

8. THOMAS WATSON: THE LAST ROMAN CATHOLIC BISHOP OF LINCOLN

John Wilford was born in Kettering in 1940. He left school in 1955 to work in the boot and shoe industry. In 1963 he returned to full-time education before commencing studies for the priesthood in a Catholic Seminary. Leaving the seminary in 1969 he married in 1970 and went to the University of Bristol to study Church History and Theology. He graduated in 1974 and began a career in archaeology and part-time lecturing in Lincoln. In 1990 he was elected a Fellow of the Society of Antiquaries.

He retired from archaeology to be ordained Deacon in 1997. He is now Roman Catholic Chaplain to the University of Lincolnshire and Humberside.

9. TECHNICAL EDUCATION FOR LINCOLN – 'A CITIZENS' UNIVERSITY'

Jan Relf has taught British and French eighteenth and nineteenth century history at North Lincolnshire College since graduating from the University of Humberside in 1995 with a BA (Hons) in Literary and Historical Studies. She gained a PGCE in Further Education in 1997 at the Nottingham Trent University.

Prior to teaching she spent some ten years in commerce and business before embarking on a business partnership with her artist husband producing historical relief carvings and artefacts for museums, galleries and cathedrals in Britain and America.

Her interest in education stemmed from training staff, teaching her two sons and designing and teaching Adult Education courses for mature students.

She is a keen researcher and a member of the Historical Association and Family History Association, where she recently found that she was a descendant from French Huguenots and a nineteenth century German immigrant.

10. AN 'EDGE-LAND: THE DEVELOPMENT OF THE WITHAM VALLEY, EAST OF CANWICK ROAD

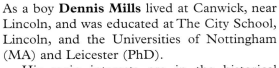

As a boy **Dennis Mills** lived at Canwick, near Lincoln, and was educated at The City School, Lincoln, and the Universities of Nottingham (MA) and Leicester (PhD).

His main interests are in the historical geography of rural Britain in the Victorian period, and he is currently working with his wife, Joan Mills, on the history of the Sibthorp estates.

His publications include *Lord and Peasant in Nineteenth Century Britain* (1980); and he edited *Twentieth Century Lincolnshire* (1989), volume XII in the now-completed *History of Lincolnshire* series. With Professor Kevin Schurer, he co-edited *Local Communities in the Victorian Census Enumerators' Books* (1996).

Dennis Mills is a member of the Survey of Lincoln executive and is working on an historical atlas of Lincoln, in which it is intended to reprint various plans of the city, including those published by J S Padley in the ninteenth century.

11. PLEASURE EXCURSIONS FROM LINCOLN 1846-1914

Eleanor Nannestad was brought up in North Hykeham, near Lincoln. After gaining a BA (Hons) in French Studies at the University of Lancaster, she took a postgraduate librarianship course at Aberdeen, then returned to work for Lincolnshire Library Service, where she now has responsibility for the Local Studies

Collection at Lincoln Central Library.

In 1990, she was awarded the University of Nottingham Certificate in Local History, with distinction, for which she presented a dissertation on Victorian pleasure excursions.

A member of the Society for Lincolnshire History and Archaeology, she has contributed to their journal, *Lincolnshire History and Archaeology* and to their quarterly publication, *Lincolnshire Past and Present.*

12. LINCOLN'S CINEMAS IN THE TWENTIETH CENTURY

George Clarke was born in Lincoln in 1920. He saw his first film in c1928. The possibilities of a future career in the media caught his fancy.

He sought and found employment in this field of entertainment. This was terminated at the request of His Majesty during the Second World War when he embarked on a world tour. Through his war service, he examined a number of continental film projectors and the cinemas that housed them. This was to prove an advantage when he returned to civilian life.

After arriving home in Lincoln, it was a shock to find that both the Plaza and Central cinemas had been lost.

He worked for a while at the Ritz Cinema, before moving to the Radion in 1948, where he worked until its closure in 1960. His remaining working years were spent as manager of a photographic retail firm.

In his leisure time, he was involved in the formation of the Lincoln Cine Section at the local Photographic Club.

During his retirement, he has collected information relating to Lincoln's cinema history, much of which he has passed to the Mercia Cinema Society.

INDEX - PEOPLE

INDEX - PLACES
Lincoln and Lincolnshire